'The life of Kathleen Lucas can (remarkable. As you turn the pages (down the passage of time with Kathleε.. ,ʊʊ, ʊwn life will be challenged by an ordinary girl from Dagenham who accomplished extraordinary feats for her God. Kathleen's story can only inspire you to higher heights as you read of the depths of her experience with God and the land to which she was called. I recommend this book to everyone who wants to be encouraged in their own walk with God.'

Paul Alexander PhD., President of Trinity Bible College and Graduate School, Ellendale, North Dakota / Carol Alexander PhD., Dean of the Graduate School at Trinity Bible College and Graduate School, Ellendale, North Dakota

Reading Kathleen's beautiful story I see a lady who was full of determination. Neither cockroaches or rebels could deter the passion in her heart to make a difference. Despite gun point situations and thefts, she remained steadfast to the call on her life. Kathleen's reflections show God's provision and protection throughout her life. She chose the call over convenience and followed the steps that God had laid out ahead of her. I pray that as you read this book, you will be challenged and inspired to lay your life down for the gospel and say "yes" to God's plans for your life.

Becky Murray, One By One Founder & CEO

The real life stories of the sacrifice, commitment and influence of missionary heroes challenge and inspire us to make a difference in our lives too. This book will do that for you.

Gary & Marilyn Skinner, Founders of Watoto Childcare Ministries and Watoto Church, Kampala, Uganda

Reading some of the stories whilst picturing Kathleen's stature made me feel very inadequate! What a woman! Kathleen is and remains a giant in faithfulness, a woman of remarkable courage who had to fight malaria, and risk her life in some terribly dark areas of the world where strong men may have fled. In the Congo Kathleen's home was often in danger from rebels and their threats. Rwanda was a dangerous place and some missionaries died, martyred for Christ. Enduring mosquitos, extreme weather, roads not fit for travel, languages to learn - are things most of us do not need to confront, but Kathleen spent 34 years with just one aim – to let people know of Jesus - whatever the cost. People like her are like those referred to in Hebrews 11:38 "the world was not worthy of them". Reading of Kathleen in this book will inspire you, humble you and hopefully challenge you, to believe that God is not looking for a "great you" but a "surrendered you" because there are more stories waiting to be written, for the glory and praise of God.

Alan Hewitt, author of 'The Gender Revolution'

In a courageous and gripping manner, Kathleen handholds you through the terrifying and complex sociopolitical times of eastern DRC and the Great Lakes region in the 1950's and 60's. Very little is known or written about the work, experiences and impact of missionaries in that part of DRC to the breadth and depth that Kathleen openly shares in her book. She offers a reader an unfiltered and authentic close up account of a lived experience. It's as challenging as it is inspiring. Kathleen's adorable traits of bravery, endurance and dedication represent the power of faith and God's love for a woman who simply chose to say 'yes' to Jesus.

Solomon Mugera, Director of Communications and External Relations for the Africa Development Bank Group and former head of BBC Africa, BBC World Service

From Dagenham to Africa with love

The Story of One Woman's Decision to Say "Yes" to Jesus

Kathleen Lucas

Written by Hannah Williamson

Dedicated to...

This book may be an account of my experiences but, in reality, it is a story of the faithfulness of God and the many pastors and churches who supported me financially and practically over the 34 years - and also to the various missionary secretaries from Assemblies of God and pastors who arranged itineraries, opened their homes to me, offered accommodation and in the early days even transported me to my next appointment or to the rail or bus station.

My thanks to all who wrote encouraging letters, made up food and clothing parcels, and encouraged Sunday school children to give their puzzles and board games to occupy students in their free time.

I would like to dedicate this book to every person I had the honour of partnering with both on the mission field in The Congo and Rwanda and those from the UK, Sweden and many other parts of Europe.

Kathleen Lucas

Contents

Acknowledgements

I firstly want to say thank you to Kathleen for being willing to share her story. I am sure there are so many men and women, heroes of the faith who don't share their stories with the world. I know for Kathleen the experience of writing her story was not always the easiest, having to relive times in her life on the mission field that were painful and traumatic. Thank you for allowing me to sit with you and listen and write. It will always be one of the greatest honours of my life.

Thank you to my Mum, Christine Williamson who sat with Kathleen and I for every session that I listened to Kathleen tell her story. Mum was able to prompt questions to help us ensure we had everything written down.

Thank you to those who have helped me by checking names of places, ensuring we have correctly recorded historical events and checking all things grammar related. Thank you to Eileen Riordan for hours spent reading over the manuscript. Thank you also to Solomon Mugera who I know checked the manuscript despite his hugely busy schedule as director of communications and external relations for the Africa Development Bank Group. We so appreciate you taking the time to do this and bringing your expertise on East Africa.

Finally, and most importantly, I want to thank God for helping us to get this story down on paper. There were times as we sat with Kathleen where the presence of God was so tangible. This is a story of someone who gave their entire life for His service. This is a God story!

Hannah Williamson

Forward

'Then I heard the voice of the Lord saying, "Whom shall I send? And who will go for us?" And I said, "Here am I. Send me!"' Isaiah 6:8

A s the Mission's Director for Assemblies of God Great Britain (AOG GB), some of the most life changing occasions happen when I am able to meet, hear and learn the stories of our missionaries on the field. I always leave those encounters with a deeper understanding of the heart and power of God and how God uniquely calls and graces His servants in His mission to the nations.

AOG GB has an incredible history of sending missionaries to the nations and establishing churches, hospitals, schools, bible colleges and other expressions of mission that have transformed communities. Hannah Williamson has been able to take the story of one of our heroine missionaries of AOG GB, Kathleen Lucas and bring it to life. Hannah has been able to articulate Kathleen's mission story in a way that I felt as if I was in the lounge room as Kathleen recounted her experiences of God's call, provision, miracles, opportunities and protection over the 34 years of mission service on the field in Africa.

I remember meeting Hannah Williamson in 2019 in the church at Dagenham, which much of Kathleen's story is intertwined with. I was aware of Hannah's reputation of being a young missional leader with a passion and tenacity to reach those who did not know Jesus. Hannah's heart for mission and personal relationship with Kathleen is so evident in her writing, that you will have a front row seat in the story of Kathleen's life. Hannah has also captured the historical, geographical and political climates that Kathleen served in and through. I am so thankful that Hannah took the time to interpret Kathleen's story, it is both a gift to me and to the AOG GB family.

Today the mission of AOG GB is called 3Dmissiongb, where the three D's stand for Discover, Develop and Deploy. Through reading Kathleen's story on the following pages you will see clearly how Kathleen discovered God's call for her life; how she developed it and how she was deployed to the nations. This book will give you personal insight into the life of a missionary that is not always heard, including both the supernatural miracles and the personal sacrifices.

At times when reading about the political and violent trouble in both the Congo and Rwanda through which

Kathleen served Jesus, I thought I was experiencing a harrowing blockbuster movie. Yet, in the midst of such evil and terror I was in awe of Kathleen's determination to keep serving Jesus, keep saying 'yes', no matter what the cost.

In this book I was reminded that when we say yes to God, to go, to be deployed into His mission, then God will provide, God will protect and God's gospel is the power of salvation. This book reminded me of the power of God's prophetic word and the power of prayer. This book reminded me of the power of a local church that is committed to send and support a missionary as an extension of their own church in the field. May it be an example to all our AOG GB churches.

Hannah has also provided a space for personal reflection at the end of each chapter which allows you and I to pause, consider and apply the story of Kathleen to our own lives today. I pray that in these reflection moments, God will speak to your heart and mind about your own mission adventure that God wants you to have.

The question Isaiah overheard in the throne room of heaven is still the same question that resounds across the earth; "Who shall we send? Who will go for us?" This book is the story of Kathleen Lucas, who answered the same as Isaiah, "Here I am, send me." I pray that this book moves you to also be a person who says, "yes, here I am send me."

Pastor Kirk McAtear

National Leadership team/Mission Director Assemblies of God Great Britain.

Introduction

A note from the author

I grew up reading stories of missionaries who had given their lives to serve parts of the world that were relatively 'unreached' with the gospel. They were always inspiring and encouraged me in my own walk with God, challenging me when the time came to say "yes" to Jesus and follow His call to reach people with His love. When I asked Kathleen if I could write her story, she responded with such great enthusiasm saying she had hoped someone would help her with this. At the stage I was at in my own life and ministry I had a little extra time to be able to dedicate myself to this project. Little did I realise how transformative it would be for me. I had anticipated being inspired as I had grown up hearing Kathleen's stories although I now realise I had only ever heard a tiny portion of them. I was personally at a crossroads in my own ministry, seeking God for my next steps. My weekly times with Kathleen will stay in my memory as a part of my journey in stepping out in faith to do what God called me to.

For six months, most weeks (partly on FaceTime during the covid outbreak - we managed to teach Kathleen how to FaceTime, at age 87!) I would sit with Kathleen and my mum, typing as she dictated her story to me. I soon realised that I had gone into this project somewhat naively, initially thinking that Kathleen would tell me a few stories and I would form them into a written story. Kathleen, however trawled through hundreds of letters that she had written to her mum while she was on the mission field. She would then handwrite in a notebook her story and dictate it to me. Although there was a huge level of documentation, I was always amazed at Kathleen's ability to remember the names of each individual, and the details of each place she recalled.

I certainly did not realise how difficult and at times traumatic it would be for Kathleen reliving what she went through on the mission field. She shared stories that I believe she had never told anyone. Many are in this book, some are not. I will always be grateful that Kathleen trusted me with such information and allowed me a glimpse of the sacrifice she gave in serving Jesus. She did it with her whole life.

Kathleen's life has been intertwined with my family for most of her life. She was very close friends with my grandparents having all grown up in the same church. I remember hearing how my mum and aunt would sit around the dining room table and listen to their mum read the letters from Kathleen on the mission field. My grandma at the time was the mission's secretary for the church I grew up in and so she wrote to Kathleen in that capacity and as a friend every month. There are many photos of my grandparents meeting Kathleen at the station when she arrived home on furlough.

When I was born in 1984, Kathleen was beginning her work in Rwanda and had already spent a considerable amount of time on the mission field, having gone through a great deal in the Congo. Most of my memories of Kathleen have been as a teenager and into my 20's when she returned home to Dagenham. Kathleen came home from the mission field in 1992 when I was just eight. She has always been my inspiration and cheerleader. Having written her story, I now understand a little more the reason she would always encourage me in my journey as a woman in ministry. I remember times when I was youth pastoring and helping boys who had joined gangs, Kathleen would ask for their names. I would only give their first names, and she would passionately and consistently pray for them, many of these boys with heritage from nations she served for most of her life. Having written her story, it has given me so much context as to why she would be so passionate about 'my boys.'

I will forever be grateful to Kathleen for giving me the opportunity to sit with her, be mentored by her and write her story. Every time I sat with her, my eyes would well up with tears as Jesus would speak to me through her story challenging me to give once again everything to Him. I hope as you read Kathleen's story you will also, like me, be challenged to reach and serve people with the love of Jesus. If God can call and use Kathleen, a relatively every day girl from Dagenham to serve Him, then He can call and use you in ways you would never be able to imagine.

Hannah Williamson

Chapter 1

Early Years

1934-1945

"The Lord himself goes before you and will be with you; he will never leave you nor forsake you. Do not be afraid; do not be discouraged." Deuteronomy 31:8

I was born on 16th January 1934 in a house in School Road in Dagenham. My parents were originally from the East End of London, having grown up in Bethnal Green. My mum, Catherine Esther Howell, was born in Whitechapel hospital and my dad, Henry Lucas in West Ham. In Bethnal Green my parents rented a room from a Mrs. Wright at 51 Lessada Street, Roman Road. At that time in the early 1900's overcrowding was increasingly a problem in the East End and so new estates were built further east to try to alleviate the problem. It was sometimes known as the 'cockney diaspora'. Particularly between the two wars, significant work was undertaken to build these housing estates, one of them being the Becontree Estate in Dagenham. My uncle and aunt had already made the move to this estate and presumably suggested to my parents that they begin looking. They moved into a new house in 1933 on the Rylands Estate in Dagenham just two months before I was born. The house cost a total of £500, and my parents had to borrow £5 for the deposit from my grandfather who was also living in Dagenham in Rugby Road. The mortgage at the time was £3.50 per month!

Prior to the war, my dad was a carpenter who specialised in cabinet making. He also made sun blinds for big shops in the area. Growing up dad had done a few other jobs, one of these being a 'messenger boy' who ran from office to office spreading messages before phones (landline phones at that time) were more available. He knew London like the back of his hand as he ran everywhere with messages!

Before marriage, mum worked for Mason Pearson Hairbrush Company. In the mid 1860's a man from Yorkshire called Mason Pearson came to work at the British Steam Brush works in the East End. In 1885 he invented the "pneumatic" rubber-cushion hairbrush which became the company's primary product and is still on sale today. Little changed from the original design of which the "Junior" model, with a mix of boar nylon bristles, was popularly known as "The Ferrari of Brushes." Mum worked in the factory making these hairbrushes. Mrs. Mason took a great interest in her workers as mum often recalled. Mum and her friends would often spend their lunch break walking by the Bryant and May matchstick firm that was close by. The East End was teeming with factories at the time. When my parents got married in the September of 1928, it was expected that mum would give up work as was so common in those days.

In 1930, my oldest brother Ronnie was born, followed two years later by my sister Edna and then me in 1934. I don't remember anything of my brother Ronnie as he sadly passed away on 17 November 1935, thirteen days after his fifth birthday and just a year after I was born. I still have a Micky Mouse children's book which was given to me from Ronnie with an inscription in it saying: 'Ronnie's last gift to Kathleen.' I later found out that Ronnie died of Streptococci although all I was told at the time was that he had a sore throat. Penicillin was invented in 1928 but not used to treat infections until 1942 and so would not have been used to treat the infection my brother caught. I remember my mum always being worried back in those days if any of us got sick with a sore throat. I know little of how mum coped although reading some accounts from other family members showed me how difficult it must have been for her. She lived with great fear of all her other children becoming ill like Ronnie. My younger brother John was born in 1939.

Although I know of little spiritual belief in my family background, I know that my mum went to Sunday School in the East End growing up. I have a book which belonged to my mum called 'The Travellers' Guide – from death to life' which has an inscription on the front saying, 'To Kate, from Dad' on 4th May 1916 which my mum would have received at the age of ten. I have also discovered a Bible that again on the inside said: 'To Kate, from Dad.' Perhaps a sign that there was a degree of faith in those early days of my family? I do wonder if my mum made a decision to follow Jesus as a child although I never knew about this. God was never spoken of in our home and so it was only when I went to Sunday School that I heard about Him.

Bible verse cards I received at Bethel Church Sunday school

When we had moved into the house in Dagenham, some church workers from Bethel Church (the Assemblies Of God church in Dagenham) came knocking on our door inviting children to Sunday School. My mum naturally sent Ronnie and Edna along, perhaps because her memories of Sunday School were pleasant. Once I was old enough I too, went to Sunday School with my elder sister Edna. I remember hearing that when Ronnie passed away, Mr. Ward who was the Sunday School Superintendent at the time, came round to visit my parents to offer his condolences and offer any support the church could give.

War Years

War broke out in September 1939, nine months after my youngest brother John had been born. I was five years old, and my memories of this time remain vivid. Very quickly every home was to have an Anderson shelter built to protect from incoming bombs. The state provided these, but it was a rush to get them done. I remember during the first air raid, our Anderson shelter was not complete, so we had to rush next door to share the neighbour's! Fortunately, not long after, our shelter which was built for four people was completed. We had two bunkbeds on either side that were provided for us. We did, however, have to make our own straw mattresses as these were not provided. Mum and I slept on the lower bunks whilst Edna was in the higher bunk. My youngest brother John, who was still a baby, had a carry cot with a gas mask fixed into it to protect him as he was too young to have a normal gas mask. It looked like a rubber bubble with an air pump attached to it. We all had masks that we would keep with us at all times. My gas mask had 'Micky ears' which was common for children to attempt to make it a little less scary. Our gas masks were often tested at school where a 'tester' would stretch the rubber to see if there was even a tiny pin hole. I remember the fear of having a hole in mine. For some reason you felt this sense of shame that you had not looked after one of your now, most valuable items. If yours was found to have a hole, you had to go to a special place to have a patch put over it.

I will never forget that we had a 'document box' that was between the bunkbeds in the Anderson shelter which contained the deeds to the house, birth certificates and other such documents which must never be lost or destroyed if the house was bombed. We used a rather large biscuit tin as our document box to keep these items safe! There were strict rules about keeping your house blacked out and if there was any bit of light showing through, wardens would come round and instruct you to fix it. Any small amount of light could indicate where a bomb could be dropped. There were no streetlights used and so torches became vital for us during this time.

As I was five when the war started my primary school years were lived in 'wartime Britain'. I attended Marsh Green Primary School which was close to where we lived. Before the air raid shelters were built, school closed but teaching continued. In order to do this, classes were split into groups of 10 children and certain families were nominated to host lessons in their homes. Teachers were to work their way around these homes spending between one hour to one hour thirty minutes in each home teaching. I remember my sister Edna's class were to come to our house for her lessons. I was in a younger class so had to go to another home a little way up the road for my lessons. This continued for about six months although the class sizes halved once children began being evacuated.

Eventually, there was an air raid shelter built in the playground of the school which we were to go into any time we heard the signal which was a loud siren. Some of the corridors were also built with reinforcements that some classes would go into but most of my memories are in the ones that were in the playground. When there was an air raid, we would hear a loud drill that changed in sounds. This would signal that we needed to go to the air raid shelter very quickly. We were instructed to stand up, pack our books into our folders, put our gas mask on our shoulders and wait to be directed outside. Once the teacher directed us, we would follow in a line out to the air raid shelter where we would go in and sit on the benches that were provided. We were supposed to continue our classes in there although this didn't always happen! If planes could be heard while we were in there, teachers would direct us all to sing at the top of our voices in an attempt to drown out the noise of the planes and take away some of the fear that we felt. The signals for the start and for the end of the air raid were almost similar. The only difference was that the former came with varied sounds while the latter was long and continuous. This would then mean we could stand and make our way back to the classrooms to continue our learning. In those days we would normally go home for lunchtime but during the war, at times, we were told to bring in some bread or sandwiches for lunch in case it was too dangerous to walk home.

As the war began to heat up, many children were evacuated from the East End and surrounding areas into the countryside or even other countries for their safety. On 2 September 1939, a day before war was declared, 15,000 children left Barking on train journeys to Somerset. After many protests at being excluded from the scheme, Dagenham was finally declared an evacuation area in June of the following year. It hurriedly organised an ambitious scheme to move its children by water. By 3rd September, 17,000 had boarded paddle steamers at Ford's jetty for their journey to east coast ports at Lowestoft, Felixstowe and Yarmouth. My mum didn't want us to be evacuated, wanting to keep us all together and so we lived through the war in our home in Dagenham. I wonder now if this had anything to do with her losing her firstborn, Ronnie. The fear of losing any of us was too great for her to handle and so keeping us close seemed like a better option despite the danger. I also wonder now if this was a challenge for her when I went off to the mission field especially considering there would be times when she would be unsure if she would ever see me again!

I will always remember our first Christmas during the war in school. There was a lovely Christmas tree with gifts underneath which were to be given to certain children. I had spotted a beautiful doll and really hoped she would be given to me, but it was not to be. She was given to a child who was to be evacuated to Canada.

We were all given identity cards which the adults had to keep on them at all times. Mine was CCKO1604. Everyone in the family had a similar number but for the last digit. Dad had 1601, mum 1602, Edna 1603 and presumably my younger brother John being 1605. Ration books were also a common part of life and were used for everything including food and clothes. I remember times we would get eggs from the shop and when it came time to use them, we would crack them into a bowl but if they were off, I was given the task of taking the bowl with the 'gone off' egg back to the shop to prove it was no good in order to get a new egg. This was how valuable food was back then.

There were certain foods that we stopped being able to get that were imported from other countries such as bananas. In fact, we used to sing a song that went, 'Bananas! Yes, we have no bananas today!' We had to use other ways of getting food due to a severe shortage and so most people grew vegetables in their gardens or allotments. Our diets were simple back then as we were making use of any food we could find! I remember we kept rabbits as pets, but it was normal for us to have to say 'goodbye' to them as they were taken by the next-door neighbour who would skin and cut them ready for us to eat!

Halfway through the war there was an exciting moment where we were allowed to get an orange each. Many such fruits were no longer being imported and so were rare to come by! I remember being quite excited by this treat. Items such as sugar and butter continued to be rationed well after the war as I remember being at college and having a certain amount allocated to me.

I have strong memories of the blitz. At that time my father had not yet been called up to serve. They called up the younger men at the start and so I remember that when the blitz came dad was still with us. We went outside into our garden and looked up to the very red sky. I remember my dad saying: 'that's London gone!' A sad and confusing day indeed! When dad was called up to service, we were all in the same room in the house. I remember saying goodbye, not knowing when we would see him again but just having to accept that this was the way life was. Dad became part of the Marines and was posted initially to Chatham. Dad travelled extensively during the war, beginning in South Africa, and working his way up through the African continent and then into Italy and eventually Belgium. Little did he know that I would embark on a similar journey when I was called to missions' work in Africa. Dad would sometimes come home to visit when he was back for signal training, and I remember him sitting at the table in the kitchen learning the morse code as this was the role he played within the war efforts.

Bethel Church sent parcels to men who were serving on the frontline and my dad received one of these even though he never attended church. I guess that my involvement through the Sunday School opened a door for the church to show this kindness to him. The parcels contained food and toiletries along with a New Testament pamphlet and other reading material to encourage the men. This obviously meant a great deal to my dad because when he returned from the war, he asked to come to church with me to show his gratitude.

Copies of the "Soldiers, Sailors and Airmen's Guide" were purchased for distribution among the armed forces. The booklets made clear the way of salvation and were attractive in their format. The Pastor's address was printed in them so that the men could ask for help and further information.

Sunday School continued during the war. Mr. Ward who ran it would say "as long as there are children, Sunday School continues!" If there was an air raid during Sunday School, we would pile into the Anderson shelter in the nearby park to continue with our learning. Anyone from the park who was in the shelter also got to be part of the Sunday School.

One morning, early in the war, we were told to evacuate our home very quickly. An unexploded bomb had come down as part of a parachute and had got trapped in someone's chimney in Review Road, not far from where we lived. Mum had a friend in Goresbrook Road, a little further away so we quickly made our way there. A bomb disposal team were called to try to diffuse the devise but unfortunately it went off killing all those around. From where we were in Goresbrook Road we could see the black smoke rising. My dad said, 'That's our house gone' but when we got back our house was still intact although many houses around had smashed windows. The only thing that had happened to our house was that the roof hatch had completely turned over! Just down the road from us, which became the talk of the town, a lawnmower had flown across a few houses into another garden, such was the extent and power of the blast!

At another point another bomb went off in Ford Road which was again not far from us. All the neighbours went out to see the damage. I remember as a child watching families just standing in shock looking at the devastation. I saw the boot of a small child and remember the shock, and sadness that this caused me as I realised what had happened to that child. Bombing was normal and I remember later into the war that the 'doodlebug' came with vengeance. These were self-driven bombs, and you could hear them coming. Although there was great fear, there was a sense amongst people that you just had to try and survive.

There were constantly bits of parachute and shrapnel left on the streets from fallen and exploded bombs. There was a lady on our road who collected the nylon from the parachutes and made them into miniature parachutes that she gave to children in the street to play with. We often collected bits of shrapnel as there was a need for metal. You could hand this in to be reused. We were later forbidden to do this in case it caused harm. Later in the war, there was also fear about what was being picked up by children as there were miniature explosives that were dropped and hadn't exploded. Of all the different types of bombs, we were most fearful of the vengeance bombs as these were the silent ones that killed thousands.

Although there were many bad memories from the war days, there were good ones too like the time we managed to get away on holiday. My uncle had been working in Sheerness in the dockyard and was able to arrange for us to visit. It was common that you were allowed to travel around freely in those days but in order to go to the dockyard you had to have special permission. My uncle managed to get us this special permission because we were 'poor blitz children' so we had a wonderful time together by the sea!

Sunday School
Sunday school during the war was also a great highlight for us as children. There were Christmas parties, annual prize-givings, sandwiches, wonderful trifle and jelly! We would sing together. But when I look back, I'm struck at how strange some of the songs were, especially considering so many of the children were not from church backgrounds. One song I especially remember went, 'Rout them out, bid them gone, all the little bunnies in the fields of corn. Envy, jealousy, malice and pride, don't let these bunnies in your heart abide.' Seeing as we had bunnies at home, I wasn't

sure what this song meant and certainly didn't understand words like envy and pride! There were also Sunday School outings in the summer as long as it was safe to travel. We would meet at Dagenham East train station where we caught a train to Upminster and then to Leigh-on-Sea to spend the day at the beach! Many children from the community attended these outings. We would always have tea at 4pm in the local café which was always a highlight of the trip.

Mr. and Mrs. Ward who ran the Sunday school and organised all the outings were outstanding people of faith. There were times when more than 300 children turned up and this couple prayed for each child individually. They did so daily. I was a very regular attender of the Sunday School and eagerly got involved in church activities. On a Wednesday I would attend the Children's Bible Club where I began to learn the stories from the Bible that I would not have encountered at home. I also went to a sewing club at the church where we would make items which could be sent to the mission field to support those in need. It was here that I first heard of people who served God in other parts of the world. I was so involved as a child that at times Mr. Ward would allow me to have the key to the church. My duty was to open the building and prepare for the Bible club before he got there after coming back from work. I always saw this as a great honour! I do remember Mr. Ward one day telling me that I was 'quite a chatterbox!'

VE Day

On 8th May 1945 when I was aged 11, the end of the war was announced and VE day took place. I should have been receiving my 11+ exam results on that day but due to the excitement the results of the exams came a little later! Dad wasn't home from the war at this stage, but my aunt and uncle and their 5 year old son came early in the morning to see my mum. They wanted to go to London to celebrate along with a million other Londoners! They chose to take their 5-year-old son and my brother John with them but for some reason my sister and I were left behind. Maybe it would cost too much to take us, so we were left at home to have our own celebration. Whilst mum was out, we noticed that not far from School Road where we lived people had collected logs that had been cut down for the war effort and had piled them up together in the street and created a massive bonfire. After years of having to live in darkness, light was formed in places throughout London to celebrate! People were sitting around singing, laughing and rejoicing that the war had finally come to an end. My sister and I snuck out to be part of the celebrations although a neighbour who knew our mum eventually told us to go home when it began getting late!

One of the biggest lessons I learnt during the war was 'making use of anything you had' because we did not have so much at that time. This prepared me practically for my time on the mission field when I would have to use so many things in order to help others. It also built a resilience in me that prepared me for the future. Time and time again we would have to 'leave suddenly' on the mission field due to

My primary school report

threats and risk of death. In the war years we were required to have gas masks at school every day and had to learn to always be prepared. I became 'used to' the idea of evacuation! Even when back and itinerating, I would always have my passport with me! This was something learnt from the war as we always had to have our identity cards with us. I was so used to carrying everything I might possibly need. Even now, I still carry a card with my blood type on!

Dad's release form from Naval Service

The 11+ exam results came 2 days after VE day on 10th May 1945. At the end of term, if we had good results it would mean we could enter grammar school. In celebration of receiving good results my parents bought me a brand-new leather satchel. They were extremely proud of me for doing so well in school. This satchel was later passed down to my brother John.

Dad was still abroad in Belgium when VE day came. He was officially released from service in October 1945.

Reflect...

Having read about Kathleen's early years, reflect on how your own early years have shaped you?

Are there any experiences you faced that helped prepare you for your future?

Chapter 2

Rich, Formative Years

1945-1957

"You did not choose me, but I chose you and appointed you so that you might go and bear fruit —fruit that will last..." John 15:16

This season of my life was full of the testimonies and autobiographies of missionaries who had gone before me – a preparation for what was to come.

At the end of the war, gifts were sent to the mission field and dad helped me to prepare a parcel that was to be sent to Sierra Leone. I still have the address we were given to send to 'Fatu Kagbo, care of Miss F Ruck, U.P. Mission,

Gbinti via Port Loko, Sierra Leone.' Dad helped me to repair fountain pens that I had collected and stubs of pencils, and other odds and ends that could be sent abroad.

Missionary Inspiration

During my time at Sunday School, I often heard of the work of missionaries and occasionally, missionaries would come and visit us when they were on furlough. Their visits were always so inspiring. There are some stories that have stuck in my mind such as Mr. Francis from China who visited the church. He was a great inspiration to me. He spoke of a time when he was in China and his wife had given birth to a child and they needed an incubator. There were no planes flying and there wasn't even a landing strip planned but they heard a plane coming so they went out and began waving. Miraculously, despite there not being a landing strip, the plane descended into an open area and asked what the trouble was. They responded that they were desperately in need of an incubator. The crew of the plane said, 'your prayers have been answered'! They had an incubator that was being transported from one hospital to another. God had answered their prayers! This story would stick with me and be of comfort to me, when years later I found myself under house-arrest walking around a garden wondering if we would ever be rescued. I would look up to the sky and say to God 'You did it for Mr. Francis and so you can do it for me.'

On one occasion the local Parish church had a missionary from China who was showing slides on a magic lantern.

Magic lanterns were a very simple form of projector showing slides and I found his pictures fascinating!

By now sewing classes had been introduced at Bethel for children and teenagers. It was fully operational with Mrs. Howard teaching young girls how to hand stitch garments that were to be sent abroad for distribution on the mission field. The book about Bethel Church[1] states, 'Interest in missionary work had always been encouraged even among the young. A girls' sewing class was held each week where garments were made for the needy in other lands. Bill Davis was missionary secretary at this time and he, together with a small team, used to paste texts in various languages into used Christmas cards. These were used as a means of spreading the Gospel in other lands. In 1950, 11,000 cards were sent together with 100 bandages. In 1952, 50,000 were sent in 13 languages.'

Filled with the Holy Spirit & Baptism in Water
In August 1947, as Mr. Ward was leaving work, the Lord prompted him to come to the sewing class and speak to the girls about the Baptism in the Holy Spirit. He arrived and said he wanted to pray with us. He told us that the Holy Spirit was a gift from God and all we had to do was reach out and accept the gift. He brought along a peach to illustrate the point. This was the first time I'd ever seen a peach as they were not very common then. He said, 'What do you have to do to have a bite of this peach?' Of course I

---

[1] **75 amazing years, 2002, Christine Williamson**

said, 'Take it!' He told me to get on my knees, he began to pray and I asked for the Holy Spirit and from that day on I began to speak in tongues. I was 14 at that point. As we knelt in prayer, I began to praise the Lord in other tongues and a flood of peace came upon me, my praise to God and the anointing of God was abundant. That was three weeks after my youngest sister Rona was born on 31 July 1947. I was so overcome by the Holy Spirit that I just could not stop speaking in tongues. I remember walking home and just walking around the streets for hours praying and speaking in tongues. Eventually when I finally arrived home, my older sister, Edna, was not too happy that I had been out for so long! She was unaware of the encounter I had had with the Holy Spirit that had prevented me coming home on time!

A year later, I was baptised in water at Bethel Church where there was a baptismal pool under the platform. We wore swimming hats to keep our hair dry although one man in the church told me I wasn't properly baptised as I hadn't got my hair wet – I didn't worry too much about his comments! We definitely went under the water! We had to wear white gowns which was quite common in churches in that era. To stop them from billowing out too far we had sand or coins in the hems! Our church had sand because it was cheaper than the coins! It was strange as we were not encouraged to invite our family to see our baptism at the time. I had to ask for a towel, so mum knew what was happening but unfortunately didn't come along to witness this special moment for me. Our pianist at the time chose a chorus for each baptismal candidate. The song chosen for me had the words: 'Follow, follow, I will follow Jesus. Anywhere, everywhere, I will follow on. Follow, follow, I will follow Jesus. Anywhere he leads me I will follow on.' In many ways this was a prophetic statement of what was to come in my life.

Those who Inspired me to the Mission Field

We were encouraged to read biographies of not only Bible characters but the testimonies of others. What a wealth of inspiration and encouragement there was to draw upon! The Word of God tells us to draw on the examples of others, observe their love for the Lord and learn how to avoid the pitfalls they fell into. Hudson Taylor (1832-1905) who founded the China Inland Mission and was on the mission field for 51 years, was a great inspiration to me. The life of Hudson Taylor taught me that you can't out-give God. Whilst a student, he was asked by a child to come and pray for his sick mother. When he saw the squaller and hunger that had overtaken this family he was moved to help. He only had a small amount of money in his pocket, of which he was prepared to give half, but he'd only got the one coin. It was what he had to live on for food and rent for a month, but the Lord was prompting him to give it. He had a little battle with the Lord but finally yielded to the Lord's prompting and gave it all. When he returned to his lodgings his landlord gave him an envelope and someone had anonymously given a gift which was twice the amount he had given. He declared, 'God's bank gives greater dividends than man's bank.' He also, whilst on the mission field, found that fellow workers would ask him to pray for them. He agreed but told them 'God will answer your prayers as well as mine.' I will always remember reading these stories and the great impact they had on me, inspiring me in the years to come.

Gladys Aylward (1902-1970) was another missionary to China who I read about and was inspired by. She fascinated me with her account of the Inn of 7th Happiness. Her faith and the way she smuggled children to safety in coal trucks – what a testimony! To me her tenacity and faith were infectious.

Francis Ridley Havergal (1836 – 1879) was another great inspiration. She was an English poet and hymn writer. She was taught by her mother to pray: 'prepare me for all that you have prepared for me.' That was certainly a prayer I prayed!

I read the book 'Uncle Tom's Cabin; Life Among the Lowly', by Harriet Beecher Stowe (1811-1896) which was a classic example of God's leading, provision and care. The story was an anti-slavery novel which is said to have helped lay the groundwork for the American Civil War. I happened to read Harriet Beecher Stowe's biography. She was an American abolitionist and author. Little did I know the pain and agony that she experienced whilst she was writing of the beatings and ill treatment that Uncle Tom received at the end of his life when he was bought by another slave owner. She suffered weeks of pain, sickness and agony whilst writing. It struck me that she had to live the pain in order to write it!

The Call to the Mission Field

The day after I left school at the age of 16, there was a meeting to be held at Barking Elim church with a guest speaker from South Africa called David du Plessis. He was known as 'Mr Pentecost' because he always spoke on the baptism of the Holy Spirit. In one of the meetings they sang a song that said, 'Lord, send me, here am I, send me. I want to be greatly used by thee. Across the street or across the sea, here am I my Lord, send me.' The song was sung over and over and then an appeal was made for anyone willing to say 'yes' to the call of Jesus. I stood up and said 'yes.'

On the Monday after this encounter with God's will for my life, I started work at an office in an insurance company in London near Monument, working there for three years. Toward the end of the third year there, I began to think about what I was going to do about the missionary call I had received. I knew I had to do something, so I spoke to Alfred Webb, my pastor at the time about going for nursing training. By this point It would have been Christmas 1953. I said to Alfred Webb, 'I'm going to write to find out about nursing training.' He asked 'why' and so I replied, 'to prepare for the mission field.' I remember him saying to me, 'You need to think about it some more because they are not sending single women to the mission field anymore. Pray about it for the next 3 months and then begin to think about what you should do.' Alfred Webb didn't want me to do anything impulsive as he was going to America for three months, so he wanted me to wait until he had come back.

In that period, there was such a demand for teachers. It was five years after the war. The year after the war ended became known as the 'year of the bump' because so many women got pregnant. A few years down the line, there was a shortage of teachers because of the large number of children ready to begin school! Many of the schools had been bombed and so there was a great need for new schools and more teachers. This caused a great deal of talk around the recruitment of teachers. I was more and more confused, convinced it was nursing that was the route for me but aware of the need for teachers. One morning I said, 'Lord, if you want me to be a teacher, give me a sign today.' I went off to the office. There had been so much conversation for a long time about the need for teachers, but nobody spoke about it on that day. It was a Thursday and so Joyce Vickers a close friend of mine and I used to meet at the Heathway after work and go on 'doorbell evangelism', inviting people to church. I was convinced she would speak about it but she said nothing. We bought a bar of chocolate which would be our tea on the way to the bible study at church. Alfred Webb was now home from his American trip. He had been in Colchester at a meeting the night before and had stayed overnight with a host family. As they were getting ready for the morning the lady said she was a teacher in a local school and asked if Alfred would come and speak at the morning assembly. He agreed to do this and, in the evening, when he started his bible study, he said, 'If there is one thing I've not done in the whole of my ministry life, it is that I've not encouraged anyone to go into the teaching profession.' It was the sign from God that I needed! When I got home from the bible study, I wrote a letter to the Dagenham education office which was situated at the Heathway, offering my services as a teacher. Within a few weeks, after the Easter holidays, I was an untrained teacher, teaching in Hunters Hall school. I taught there for a few months before going on to teacher training college.

Teacher Training

I went to train to be a teacher at St Gabriel's Training College for women teachers between 1953 and 1955. St Gabriel's was a Church of England college that was founded in 1898 and was situated in Camberwell on the edge of a small park. We were given a college letter on arrival which had some words from the principal but also included various thoughts and stories from former students. On page six of the book, there was a story of a woman who had attended the school in 1913 and went to Africa as part of the university mission work. She went out to the Tanganyika territory, which is now Tanzania, not far from where I would one day go! One phrase in the writing stood out which said, 'If it is your call, it is the happiest life in the world!'

The course entailed a great deal of practical work. We were expected to make our own equipment for our time on school practice, especially for physical education. My father, being a cabinet maker, gave me many useful tips. These skills would come into action later down the line in Africa.

Another skill that I learnt at this point which came in use in my time in Africa was how to make exercise books and prepare them by using needle and thread rather than staples.

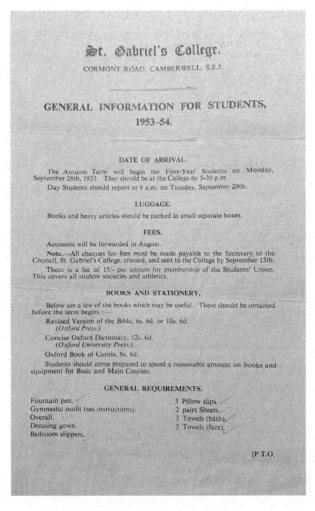

A page of the information booklet that was given to students

I amassed a great number of books and other practical materials whilst at college. Ken Thompson who was a close friend from Bethel Church declared that if he passed his driving test in time he would come and take me home with all of my goods. True to his word, the day before I left college, Ken passed his driving test! He came, piled all my goods in his car and we travelled back home. Ken and his wife Edith were great friends who faithfully supported me all throughout my journey. Not only the journey home in the car but beyond and into Africa!

College days behind me, I was engaged as a teacher in Henry Green Primary School in Green Lane, Dagenham. Two

Henry Green Primary School teacher (I am on the front row on the far right)

happy profitable years were spent there before I went to Belgium for the obligatory colonial course.

Reflect...

What 'heroes of faith' have had a great influence and impact on your life?

What are you doing or have done that is preparing you for God's next part of his plan for your life?

"She had to live with pain, in order to write it!" Has there been any pain in your life which you are now able to use the lessons learnt in that experience with which to bless others?

Chapter 3

Enroute to Africa via Belgium

1957 - 1958

'In vain you rise early and stay up late, toiling for food to eat— for he grants sleep to those he loves.' Psalm 127:2

T he Congo belonged to Belgium at this point in time (it had since 1885 when King Leopold of Belgium took the territory) and so any teacher, nurse or doctor wanting to go on the mission field there had to go on the colonial course. We had to spend nine months in Brussels, Belgium, doing a French course followed by six weeks training in teaching. Nurses and doctors had a shorter language course and then went off to Antwerp for a tropical medicine course. The Belgian government insisted that we took this before going to the Congo. There were many mission's groups that came onto this course from all over Europe.

Belgium

This was my first time leaving the UK in 1957 and it was only 12 years after the end of the war. I travelled on my own and remember being buoyed up by the prayers of others. Although there may have been some nervousness, especially travelling on my own, I had decided to go and so that's what I did! Items were quite expensive in Belgium as a result of it being so soon after the war, so I had to take as many toiletries and other items that I would need for the year as I possibly could. Many of these I had sent out ahead of me in a trunk. I travelled out to Dover and then out by ferry to Ostend and then got the train up to the Gare du Nord train station in Brussels. When I left London, my friends Joyce and Peter Vickers came to wave me off.

At this point I could speak very little French, so the language was a struggle! Mr. Woodford, the Assemblies of God (AOG) missionary secretary had arranged accommodation for me at a nurse's hostel in Brussels - the idea being that I could practice French on any willing Belgium nurse at mealtimes!

I always thought I would end up in China but at that time in AOG, no missionaries were being sent to China due to many missionaries being expelled from the country because of the victory of the Chinese communist army in 1949 and the suppression of religion. There was a great emphasis from

Joyce & Peter Vickers waving me off on my
journey to Belgium

the AOG on mission's work in the Congo and Japan. While
at teacher training college I wrote to CEM (The Congo
Evangelistic Mission, founded by William F.P. Burton and
James Salter) without any advice from anyone. They told me
to finish my training and apply afterwards. CEM was made
up of Elim, AOG and other interested missionary
associations.

Fortunately for me, when I arrived at the nurse's home Heather Atkinson, a CEM missionary candidate was already at the nursing home so my initiation to Belgian life was cushioned. She and her sister who was a nurse both went out to the Congo at the same time. They were both from the Preston AOG church. A few weeks after being in the hostel we went along to the Protestant Mission headquarters - an office that dealt with all missionaries being trained in Belgium. We went to register through them for the colonial course. They advised us to seek accommodation with a local family rather than the poor nurses! Pastor Odier rented a large room to us. Heather and I enjoyed our time with the family in Uccle.

Heather & Muriel Atkinson

My first meal in the home presented a problem for me. I was allergic to eggs and here I was being served a boiled egg on toast. We were shown into an empty dining room with two boiled eggs and toast! I remember in the young people's meetings back home, our pastor, Alfred Webb, had told us we should never be fussy about food given to us if we were invited to someone's house but should eat in faith! I looked at the egg and sighed, 'Please Lord, don't let me have any ill effects!' I was healed! I had no reaction, and this certainly helped later when I had to have a yellow fever vaccination. If you are allergic to eggs you must have a different procedure! Every time I had an egg prior to this event either boiled, scrambled or fried I vomited terribly and so this really was a miracle!

On Sundays, a group of Pentecostal students from the colonial course went to Anderlecht, another area in Brussels where Pastor Gunter originally from Peniel chapel (an AOG church in London), was now a missionary to Belgium and had planted a church in the town. Belgium insisted that if you started a church you had to do some form of social work alongside it and so this church had built a residential home for retired people. On Sundays we attended church and because it was a Flemish speaking area the service was in Flemish, translated into French by Pastor Gunter's wife, a French speaking Swiss lady. We were welcomed wholeheartedly by the church and were always invited to the evening meal with the elderly people! What a wonderful welcome we received after the service from the residents in the dining room! The residents were eager to help us with our French and so we paired up with one of them and on the one afternoon a week we had free from studies, which happened to coincide with the church's mid-week meeting we went along to the residential home and visited the elderly person with whom we were paired. We had conversation and they corrected our pronunciation, or they asked us to recite a poem we had learnt for the course or read a passage from our study book. Then they read a dictation to us from our study book! We then had to correct our own work afterwards. They were extremely helpful!

The Colonial Course

There were numerous missionaries both Protestant and Catholic attending the colonial course. The professor was extremely well organised! Because of the size of the class, he sat us in rows of about six with a designated leader at the end of each row. That leader had to keep a rota and each member of the row had to answer his questions about grammar or reading. This meant he knew that everyone was taking part and we were obliged to make progress! He was extremely strict but had little patience with the Italian nuns. They struggled to articulate certain words and no matter how much he or they tried they never agreed. Having been wounded and mistreated during the German occupation he was troubled by the presence of a German priest on the course but soon found grace to overcome his emotions and gradually a wonderful friendship was formed between the two.

Our language course was followed by six weeks of teacher training. We had courses in the history of Belgium and that of the Congo, the geography of Belgium and the Congo, hygiene and tropical diseases and the law of Belgium and the Congo. All the exams were oral. Fortunately for us, missionaries who had attended these courses over the years had remembered their questions and written them down so that we could have postcards with questions and answers. Walking to school each morning, Heather and I would ask each other questions on whatever the course was on that day.

The professor of law was a Jesuit priest. This was before the Catholic renewal (a time in the 1960's when there was a charismatic awakening amongst many Catholics. Prior to this, there were quite strong divisions between Protestantism and Catholicism) and he was very antagonistic towards Protestant candidates. He had a unique exam procedure where he took us in, a couple at a time and in alphabetical order. He would ask a question to one person and halfway through he would say 'stop' and the other one had to finish the answer! He also said: "If I raise my eyes to the heavens, YOU HAVE FAILED!" During my answers he raised his eyes to the heavens several times! Later when I recounted this to Heather, I wept. I was certain I had failed! That night, I was reading Psalm 127 and drew comfort from verse 2, which says in the amplified version, "It is vain for you to rise early, to retire late, to eat the bread of anxious labours. For He gives blessings to His beloved even in his sleep!" I slept well that night.

News About Where I Would be Going

Two Swedish missionaries, Marion Hendrickson and Rosa Carson, came to me towards the end of the course and said 'Kathleen, you're coming to work with us in Lemera. We've heard that a Baraka missionary is on loan to us for a year.' I was perplexed. I had heard nothing about this, so I just shrugged my shoulders. In August of 1958, when I visited the AOG offices in London, Mr. Woodford said to me, 'Now, when you get to The Congo (currently Democratic Republic of the Congo) you will be living in Lemera because we have promised that you can help out in the teacher training college!' Baraka, to give some context was one of AOG'S mission stations in the Congo on the lake side and the next station travelling north was Uvira and further up in the mountains was Lemera. It was the Swedish/Norwegian teacher training college. They had been told that this Baraka missionary would be on loan for a year as they needed help. They had also been accepting some of our students. When the students had gone through a teacher training course and went out to teach in the Congo their salary could be claimed from the Congolese government. Our mission had no trained teachers or registered accredited primary schools. We needed trained teachers for the primary school. It was a slow process getting one school at a time with teachers' salaries paid.

Just prior to leaving Belgium, AOG missionaries Barbara and Cyril Cross and Brenda and Geoff Hawksley had come across to Belgium for a short time to brush up on their

French before returning to the Congo after furlough. They were so encouraging! A short time later when I arrived in Congo, I spent a week with Rosalie Hegi and Barbara and Cyril Cross at Lwata, before proceeding to Lemera. Rosalie Hegi was a great inspiration. She first arrived on the mission field in 1921 and so by the time I met her she had been there for 37 years. She was an incredible woman who had been instrumental in planting over 130 churches, seeing thousands come to faith, witnessing numerous healings and training multiple Congolese people to further the work of Christ. She would often go by canoe to remote places to share the gospel where it had never been shared before.

Rosalie Hegi

I was in Belgium for a year but was able to come home at Christmas. The British missionaries had somehow arranged for tickets on a special flight. This was my first time on a plane! Ken Thompson came up to London Heathrow to greet the plane and me! I don't really remember how I felt even though it was my first time on a plane as I was just so relieved to get home and speak English! After Christmas I went back to Belgium to continue my studies.

Barbara & Cyril Cross

Assemblies of God missionaries to the Kalembelembe field from
1958 onwards

Reflect...

*So much of this chapter is about Kathleen doing things she
had never done to pursue the will of God. When was the last
time you did something for the first time?*

Chapter 4

Lemera, Congo

1958

'Remember how the Lord your God led you all the way in the wilderness these forty years.' Deuteronomy 8:2

F rom my parents' home in East London, it was always easy for me to contact the AOG missionary office in Newington Causeway in South London. As I mentioned earlier, Mr. Woodford explained that I was on loan to the Swedish mission to replace a member of staff at the teaching training college which was called IPPKi. I was the first of the Kalembelembe missionaries to travel out to the Congo by plane. At the interview I was given a list of equipment to buy to cover possible needs for the years ahead. Dad and Ken Thompson helped me to pack the reclaimed tea chest for the smaller household goods and a travel company called Allisons took charge of everything else. Prior to their return to the Congo, Barbara and Cyril Cross had been having meetings in churches in Kent talking about the work on the mission field and to encourage prayer support. They had temporary accommodation at the home of Pastor and Mrs. Pavey. Imagine my surprise when I received a letter from them inviting me for a week's holiday in this picturesque part of the country. They lived in Folkestone but were ministering in a church in Rye. The whole family welcomed me into their home and a lifelong friendship was formed. Heaven alone will reveal the extent of their generosity and sacrificial service. My flight was arranged for Sunday 9 November 1958. Mr. Woodford, the AOG mission's secretary met me at the London terminal, prayed with me and committed me to the Lord before he left to minister in one of the London churches.

The Journey to Congo

Eunice and Ken Dalrymple, church friends in Dagenham, arranged to take me to the terminal and then continue with my parents to Heathrow airport (what was then known as 'London Airport'). I had a small canvas suitcase with a zip as I thought this would make it lighter! At that time, luggage was limited to 20 kilos. It was stressed that I must take a mosquito net out with me, so this made up a significant part of the 20 kilos. The night before we had gone all the way to Dagenham Heathway with my suitcase to weigh it to ensure it would be okay and it appeared to be. All I remember thinking was, whatever happens I need to make sure I have my Bible! Alas, when we arrived at the airport, and it was weighed there I was informed that it was overweight! Shoes were the only option I could think of taking out. My dad went home with a pair of shoes to be sent by post later. A helpful airport official suggested to dad that he scratch the soles of the shoes to avoid paying customs duty on a new pair of shoes! As you will see later in my story the weight of my luggage was always a challenge when travelling. This was only my third time on a plane, but I was so preoccupied by the newness of everything that I didn't have much time to worry about going on this grand adventure on my own. I was doing what God wanted me to do and so that pushed me onwards.

By this point, mum and dad had got used to the thought that I was going to be a missionary. I know it had been quite hard for mum when I told her on my 21st birthday. I remember feeling it was like I had put a knife into her. I had felt the disappointment in my mum's face on that day, however on the day I was to fly out I began to see it replaced with pride.

I flew Air Sabena via Brussels, Athens, Cairo and then on to Stanleyville (currently Kisangani). The journey from Paris to Usumbura (currently Bujumbura) now only takes about seven hours but for me back when I was travelling, the journey started early in the morning in London, and I finally arrived the next day. All in all, it was a 2-day journey! My first night in Africa was spent in a well-equipped Congolese hotel. The final stage of my flight was by a lightweight carrier called a 'Petit Porteur' which held 10 to 12 passengers. My final stage of the flight was to Usumbura (the main port of Burundi). At that time, it was a gravel landing strip which has now been transformed into an international airport. What a joy to be met by Barbra and Cyril Cross and Rosalie Hegi. We had lunch with missionary friends, Mr. & Mrs. Hollier living in town and then went onto Uvira, in the south Kivu province which was a Swedish mission station to be greeted by Mr. and Mrs. Palmertz before continuing our journey to Nundu where two ladies Maggie Noad and Nancy Carter were stationed. Finally, we arrived in Baraka at midnight where Mr. and Mrs. Holder and Mr. and Mrs. Holland were listening to the late-night BBC news broadcast from Dar-es-Salaam in Tanganyika (currently Tanzania). When we arrived, they were listening to the news, and I was alarmed to hear Frank Holder say: 'We haven't much time left in the Congo – things are happening just as they did in China.' At the time, Belgium was beginning to lose control of the nation and there were high levels of unrest. Ivy and Frank Holder had been in China when there was trouble there for missionaries and they had to leave. I felt very uneasy and alarmed on my first night on the mission field, but that initial alarm quickly left me due to the excitement of the new experience.

During my first few days at Baraka, I was gently introduced into mission life. I went along to see the primary school with simple benches to sit on and a higher bench in front of them as a desk. The children were using slates and slate pencils. Some of them had no slate pencils so they were using small pieces of manioc root as a replacement.

I remember my walk down to the lake side (Lake Tanganyika). I was greeted by fisherman wearing long overcoats which looked like old European overcoats. My trip to Lwata later will explain the importance of these. I was impressed by the hearty singing on Sunday in the church service. They were singing in Kibembe and some in Swahili which at that time I didn't understand at all! I remember being kept awake at night by the snorting of the hippos or even the hum of mosquitoes as I lay under the shelter of the mosquito net. As an aside, before I went to the Congo, I had to have smallpox, yellow fever and cholera jabs and had to take anti malaria drugs.

Friendship on the Mission Field

Frank Holder took me to Fizi (a territory in the south Kivu province) where the district office was to register my arrival in the Congo. Once again there was a need to carry an identity card just as in Belgium. Barbara and Cyril Cross had returned to Lwata, and Rosalie and I joined them a week later. Friendship was precious in the work of God and Rosalie's friendship meant so much to me. She died in the 1980's when she was in her 80s. She really was a pioneer missionary and a mentor in missions to me. As mentioned previously, in earlier days Rosalie had often made the trip across the lake by canoe but now she owned an outboard motor driven boat. It was expertly cared for by one of her workers. About 10 of us were on board as we travelled to Lwata and as the day wore on the breeze caused the water to be quite choppy! I was being splashed and suddenly I was covered by a heavy overcoat! It was now I would learn the need for these coats to stop me being drenched by the water! The week at Lwata revealed to me how much the women especially appreciated the ministry of Rosalie Hegi and Barbara Cross. There were special women's meetings held in the church as well as informal gatherings on the steps of the houses.

Practicalities of Life at Lwata

In the absence of electricity and no running water, it was at Lwata that I learnt the importance of keeping the wicks of the lamps and paraffin fridge trimmed. This continued throughout the years I was in Congo. We only had electricity from 1980 in Rwanda! The fridges stank if the wick wasn't trimmed! There was a big tray of oil to pull out, trim the wick and make sure the oil didn't overspill as you pushed it back again. And of course, the water had to be boiled for 20 minutes before being filtered! The candles in the filter had to be cleaned regularly.

The water filter was a big container like a saucepan with a tap at the bottom, and then another balanced on top, and we had candles that were ceramic non-glazed with a tube that the water passed through and dripped through the holes in the top saucepan. It finally went into the lower saucepan having been filtered through the ceramic. They were like a candle screwed into the drum. When you cleaned them, you had to be careful to take the scum off but not the ceramic part, otherwise you would ruin it. It was quite an operation. Water, of course, was collected from the lake or in the rainy season in petrol drums from the roof. The petrol drums would be covered with a pipe coming from the roof into the petrol drum. The rest of the petrol drum was covered with material to stop leaves falling in. The water wouldn't be clean so we would sprinkle alum powder to cause the dirt to drop to the bottom of the drum - then we would have cleaner water to boil and filter.

Malaria Strikes

Returning to Baraka, Betty Holder (Frank & Ivy Holder's daughter) and I called in at the local post office to collect letters and I was glad to see that my shoes had arrived safely! I was looking forward to Christmas celebrations and especially the lake-side baptismal service, but this was not to be for me as I had a severe bout of malaria. I had only been in the country for a month! The Holders were horrified! I had done my hygiene lessons and we were given instructions as to what to take, how and how often. I said I had a certain sort of tablet but in order to counteract it I needed to take another one as well! This was according to what I'd been taught but Frank and Ivy were very concerned about this. Every time I took a pill I vomited. I was so ill, shivering (despite living in the tropics) and then hot and sweaty that I didn't know what to do with myself! I became so worn out with malaria that all I could do was just lay there. I felt so disappointed that I could not be present at the baptismal service.

On Boxing Day, the Hollands were going to Nundu. They said that they would get some suppositories to try to help but fortunately by the time they returned with them I had settled. I was living at this point in a guest house that had two rooms. The Holders were in their brick-built house, and I was in a sun brick house. We were all together in the same area but in separate homes. They brought me food and looked after me as best they could to help me recover. A conference was going on at the same time in celebration of Christmas and the baptisms. As missionaries we had no real Christmas break, things were so busy, but we did snatch a few days of break before New Year's Day. The conference was for all the Christians in the area and there were special Christmas services. For the Christians it was all about focusing on the birth of Christ as opposed to gifts and family. There were no gifts - just a special meal.

By New Year's Day, I had recovered sufficiently to be taken by the Holders up to Lemera. The road was extremely narrow, and a unique timetable had been established to get there. There were 3 hours for cars to ride up the mountain and the next 3 hours to travel down!!! This was because there were only certain points on the road where it was wide enough for 2 vehicles to pass each other. To avoid mishaps, a drum was beaten to warn that a vehicle was leaving a certain area and at the next point up the mountain a flag was waved to say there was nothing on that stretch of road and they could proceed. A flag signal showed that the road was clear, and cars could advance.

The Swedish missionaries welcomed us with open arms and showed us to our accommodation. Finally, I reached the place where I was to serve. On arrival, I noticed a letter on the table – a word of greeting from the director of the school quoting Jeremiah 29:7, *'Also seek the peace and prosperity of the city to which I have carried you into exile. Pray to the Lord for it, because if it prospers, you too will prosper.'* The warmth of the welcome that I received despite them all being strangers to me at that time made me feel like I had finally arrived 'home' to the place that God had planned.

Learning the Language

Early on the 2 January 1959, Frank and Ivy Holder returned to Baraka, and I was now a stranger in a strange land with many strange languages! At Lemera, the teacher training college, IPPKi, was founded by the joint effort of Norwegian and Swedish Pentecostal missionaries. As students graduated from the school, their qualifications gave them state recognition which meant their salaries could be paid by the state. A fund had been started by King Baudouin of Belgium between 1948 and 1955 for the advancement of the wellbeing and education of the population in the Congo. This provided for the building of the school and the administration block, the classrooms and for a dispensary. It was a large mission station and there was a very large, impressive church building and a boarding school for Swedish missionary children! Of course, there were also houses for missionary accommodation.

The first challenge that I faced was the language barrier! Students came from the whole of the Kivu province, from Rwanda and Burundi so there were roughly 10 national dialects that were represented! In the school it was obligatory to speak French but in church the message was given in Kifulero, the local language. It was also translated into Swahili which was a common language for the East of Africa right into the Congo. Swahili was a 'lingua franca' - a language used by multiple people who spoke a variety of languages in order to communicate. Swahili was often used for Arab trading so was an important language to know. In Tanganyika (currently Tanzania), Kenya and Uganda they all spoke Swahili for trade - it was known as a market language. Other languages used were Kiluba, Chiluba and Lingala which was a military language. These languages were spoken across the area because there were so many other tribes there, but they all had a grip on some form of Swahili.

The Church in Lemera

In the church you could comfortably fit 1500 people. The church, however, had a 'Big Sunday' when all the village churches around came together in the church building for the Sunday service and there could be up to 5000 represented!!! During the service we would often celebrate the Lord's Supper together.

Inside the church at Lemera

On Saturday evenings the Swedish and Norwegian missionaries had separate prayer meetings. I went to the Swedish meetings, which was a mixture of nurses, teachers and other missionaries. The language spoken was Swedish and so naturally someone would sit beside me to translate.

It was a real challenge for me back then! The conversations were very difficult to keep up with. After the meetings, I would have a 'pity party' as I couldn't understand anything!

Occasionally, I went home and felt completely cut off from people and yet at the same time knowing this was exactly where I had to be! There were times I would weep because I didn't understand anything being said. There was an elderly missionary pioneer, Linnea Haldorf who was the type of person who what she said, everyone did! I had a new camera, and she was going off for a weekend into a village. In the missionary prayer meeting I had my new camera with me rather than leaving it in the house. Linnea said, 'Give me that, I'll need it!' I was somewhat perplexed by this and didn't give it! I said 'no' and I wept that night because I was confused at why these things were being demanded of me. I found I often didn't understand what was happening or why it caused me pain.

School Days
The school followed a six-day week programme just as in Belgium, but Wednesday was a half day. Often the students and teachers would go out into the village, and we would take a storm lantern with us and our torches for the journey home. The tallest boy (although they were all quite tall in comparison to me) would carry the storm lantern on his head to show the path ahead and we would have our individual torches so that we wouldn't trip over tree roots or tread on scorpions or even possibly a snake. I often remembered the words of Psalm 119:105, *'You word is a*

lamp for my feet, a light on my path.' I had 40 students including only one girl. These students were aged 16-18 although some were a lot older who had not previously received an education and they were all training to be teachers. I taught them in French which by this point I felt fairly confident in.

My class at Lemera

My attempts at Swahili were pathetic! On one occasion I gave the young man who helped in the house a tin of black boot polish and asked him to clean the 'Viazi' which meant potatoes, instead of 'Viatu' which meant shoes! Zelma Peterson, one of the elderly missionaries and the head of station, was a real torment. She declared that she would teach me Swedish, knowing that British people have difficulty pronouncing the 'S' in Swedish. My first lesson with her was a Swedish tongue twister. It was translated 'Seven seasick seaman.' She also decided that I wasn't to have milk in my coffee as she said it was like soup! Thus, I soon learnt to delight myself with black coffee! Zelma was a gifted person - not only was she an excellent nurse but a splendid cook and extremely interested in plant life. Special birthdays were highlighted by poems composed by Zelma where she outlined something of interest concerning the life or achievements of the person you were celebrating. The poems were usually sung to the tune of a hymn. Added to Zelma's achievements was her interesting technology and gadgets. When an old telephone system was sent to Lemera, Zelma immediately mapped out the link between the dispensary at the bottom of the hill and the home of Ingegerd Rooth and Gotty Pettersson at the top of the hill. Calls for help by phone eliminated the need of a runner navigating the long route to rouse nurses during an emergency. She also organised the digging of trenches for all the wires and setting up of the phones in all the homes! The link between school and homes was also much appreciated. Zelma's teenage son delighted in performing the role of telephone operator occasionally. One day he linked my phone to Gotty Pettersson and sat back to listen to our confused reply to the calls. We would have conversations and then heard Marty's burst of laughter as he was playing a joke on us.

Entrance to the mission school at Lemera

Reflect...

Rosalie Hegi and other missionaries were a great support to Kathleen, helping her to learn and grow in the ministry God had called her to. Which people in your life have been a great help to you on your journey?

After reading the stories about the challenges with water, a lack of communication due to few telephones, what do you take for granted that you should be more grateful for?

Chapter 5

Congo Independence & the First Escape

1959 - 1961

"The Lord will keep you from all harm. He will watch over your life; the Lord will watch over your coming and going both now and forevermore.' Psalm 121:7-8

I t was in 1959 that refugees from neighbouring Urundi (now Burundi) began to arrive on the hillside surrounding Lemera. Once again, the tribal conflict between Tutsi and Hutu had caused the Tutsi to flee and find refuge in neighbouring Congo. Such was the number that the Red Cross approached the missionaries to organise the camps. Simon Pettersson, (a Swedish missionary who first went out to Congo in the mid 1950's) together with local officials allocated the sites for temporary dwellings and gardens. Machetes and hoes were distributed with orders to build a simple hut and to prepare a garden. Many were far too weak for such a task. Food and medical treatment were given by our nurses who were already situated in Lemera and later, others arrived from Sweden to ease the burden.

Families received blankets and clothing and even cooking pots to help the refugees become a little more independent. School staff helped wherever possible. As the months passed, relief containers began to arrive at Lemera. In one of the containers were several sewing machines. Ebba Hagstrand (a Swedish missionary from Burundi), saw the opportunity to open a simple domestic science class with some of the young ladies, training them and giving them valuable life skills that would help them in the future.

Graduation from School
The school year ended with the inevitable exams and school reports, but for some of the school leavers, there was the graduation ceremony and the thrill of holding a well-earned diploma. There were about 35 student teachers in my class which included only one girl. She was the first girl to have ever come to the school! We filed into the church where the graduates were congratulated by the teaching staff and decorated with floral tributes by their friends. What a joy for us to see two of the boys from the Kalembelembe field, Malanda Boniface and Jean Sulemani among the proud recipients. Tables were brought out from the dining room and a huge circle was formed on the playing field and

we all sat down to a sumptuous feast of rice and goats' meat. Lorries and vans began to arrive, and after all the celebrations, the students left for home.

Visit to Makombo & the Field Conference for Congo Missionaries

Geoff and Brenda Hawksley had invited me to visit Makombo before the annual field conference in Lulimba. During my few days at Makombo, I realised just how spoilt we were in the UK with our national health service (NHS), doctors' surgeries and hospitals. Pauline Bagshaw, who was both a nurse and midwife had a crowded schedule at the dispensary. She often had heart-rending decisions to make as I was on one occasion to witness. She was called to help an expectant mother who arrived from an isolated village. She was well overdue, and the baby was gravely deformed in the womb. At the time, the baby died in the womb and Pauline was left with the painful task of explaining to the family the procedure she needed to perform to extract the baby. This was a tough experience for me so early on in my missionary life. Prior to this I had been asked by one of the other missionaries if I wanted to attend a birth. I was eager to see this but then once I was in there, I began to feel quite faint and so they had to put me on a bed also...this had obviously prepared me for what was to come as I was able to face this difficult circumstance with Pauline.

Brenda and Geoff were well occupied with the church services, Bible studies and building work. My few days with them soon ended and we set off to Lulimba to attend the conference. This was the Assemblies of God field conference for all the British missionaries in the Congo. Maggie Noad and Rosalie Hegi were present together with Barbara and Cyril Cross from Lwata and Frank and Ivy Holder from Baraka. Hannah and Wesley Beardsmore were the conference hosts. The African pastors were headed up by Mr. Yuma. The purpose of the conference was to report on what had been happening during the year, which of the projects were moving forward and where missionaries would be placed.

There was some time for us to be ministered to whilst we were there, but the conference was more for organising what was to come. We, of course had to come together to discuss all the practicalities as there were no phones, emails, or other forms of technology available like there are today. These times of conference were a really great source of refreshment for me as I was finally able to meet with people who spoke English after many years of only being around other languages and so this was certainly a blessing.

Christmas Celebrations with Swedish Traditions
My time at Lulimba ended and I returned to Lemera to begin the new school term. As can be expected, many Swedish traditions had been introduced into life at Lemera. I had a vivid memory of 'Jul Otta' – the Christmas celebration. Early in the morning on Christmas day we had a service which ended at daybreak. It was still dark when we made our way to the church and the mountain paths were etched with pockets of light as villagers made their way to

church, each family carrying a lamp or a torch. The church was packed, carols were sung, and a vibrant message was given for this was a day of joy and thanksgiving as we remembered the glorious message of God's love to the world – Jesus our Saviour had been born. Just as the first rays of early morning light pierced the darkness, we sang the final carol and left church to celebrate in family settings. We missionaries, met together for coffee and mouth-watering cakes! It's amazing how these seemingly small things are etched on my memory!

Independence from Belgian Rule

1960 dawned! This was the year marked for the Congo to gain their independence from Belgian rule. You can see below parts of a letter I sent to Miss Copeland who was the missionary secretary in the AOG London office in Newington Causeway.

Dear Miss Copeland,

Hearty Greetings in the Name of Jesus!

June 22nd marked the close of the school year for the pupils and staff of the school at Lemera. How pleased we were to announce the last day of term and that all the students of the final year of studies had been successful in their exams. Wednesday morning the church was decorated with palm leaves and flowers in readiness for the home going service and for the distribution of the diplomas. At eleven o'clock all was arranged, the fourth-year students and the second-year students from the 'École d'apprentissage Pédagogique' filed into the church wearing new suits and dashing ties for this was the day that they had worked for and looked forward to for so many years......although this was a happy occasion one could sense a little anxiety covered the gathering. Many students were leaving school that afternoon to return to their homes not knowing what lay in store for them; the completion of their studies would be assured only by the formation of a new education authority under the control of the young Congo Republic. The thought that was dominant in the minds of our young students was the fee for the next school year. Would it be too much for them to pay?

Thursday, 30 June, the Belgian Congo became a country of the history books only. There arose in its wake a new country, completely free from the domination of Belgium and proudly bearing the name 'La République du Congo.' We had heard many stories and rumours, propagated by the locals themselves that there would be tribal wars and there could be disturbances on Independence Day. Thankfully this did not happen. We, at Lemera, were invited to participate in a great thanksgiving service conducted by the local pastors and elders of the Lemera churches. Our hearts rejoiced together with the brethren in their newly found liberty and our prayers were for the continuation of God's work in the young republic.

The service in the church came to an end and we were invited to the State building where the 'Uhuru' (a word meaning 'freedom!') celebrations were taking place. First there was a very impressive scene when all the missionaries and locals gathered around the flagstaff in front of the Bureau and at precisely eleven o'clock the new flag was hoisted into position for the first time. A beautiful flag: blue background with a central star in yellow denoting the Congo united and six smaller stars arranged by the side representing the six Congo provinces. There was a hush over the crowd and then the trumpet signal sounded. The flag slowly gained her position at the top of the flag staff and a cheer arose and for several seconds all that one could hear was the cry of Liberty 'Uhuru, Uhuru, Uhuruuuuuuuuuuuuuuuuuuuuuurrrrrrrrrrrruuuuuuu.' Hand clapping followed accompanied by tears as local people congratulated each other on their state of independence. I say that the eyes of the Congolese were filled with tears, but the eyes of the Europeans were moist too. Now that the ensign was gently floating in the breeze, official discourse began. The first person to be asked to speak was the Pastor of the Pentecostal church in Lemera. The Pastor spoke of the liberty found in following Jesus, the responsibility of a Christian and the possibilities for the Congolese now that they were free. The second person to address the crowd was a teacher who had for many years been attached to the work in the monitor school and just recently was elected the legal representative for the native Congolese church. He too had words of exhortation to leave with his audience. Finally, the king of the Wafuleros took his stand before his subjects...now was the time for the games to begin. This was particularly interesting for the missionaries for the *different villages gave demonstrations of their dances; not sexual dances but dances that are merely mimes of an animal hunt! The local scouts were invited to display their talents. I think a scout troupe in England would be surprised to see the gymnastics of their Congolese brethren but nevertheless it all helped to add to the day's celebrations .....*

Please continue in your prayers for the Congo. We anticipated difficulties on the 30th but there were none. This surely was an answer to your prayers. We expect there will be trials in the future, but He can make the rough places smoother. Praise His Name. Yours in the bond of Calvary,

Kathleen Lucas

The beginnings of unrest

While the independence day celebrations in Lemera were peaceful, we were shocked to hear of the alarming news of riots breaking out, Europeans being raped and murdered, and emergency evacuation flights being hastily arranged in Leopoldville (now Kinshasa). What a contrast to our days of celebration! Thankfully life continued to remain calm in the Kivu province at this time.

The July missionary conference this year was held in Baraka which I attended and then onto Usumbura (now Bujumbura in Burundi) to say goodbye to some Swedish missionaries leaving for furlough. The situation on our mission station was becoming uncertain. Jim Liddle, a missionary newly arrived from the UK, was also loaned to the Swedish mission to join the staff at Lemera as the situation was considered sufficiently calm. When Jim Liddle came to the Congo he arrived by boat and came in, at Dar es Salaam, the main port in Tanzania as missionaries were fleeing from the same place to take the boat home! They said to him, 'Come back with us!' but he didn't feel he should. He continued across Tanzania and came up by boat to Uvira, met by some of our missionaries and went to Baraka to meet more missionaries and then decide where he would go on to.

The new school year commenced in September but there was no news of Wilson Mutombo, a student from the CEM (Congo Evangelistic mission) field in the Katanga province. Due to where he was located it would have been dangerous for him to travel to us. We were shocked to hear of the murders of Teddy Hodgson and Elton Knauf, both CEM missionaries. Teddy was from Preston in the UK and was a pioneer missionary to the Congo who lived in the country for about 40 years. When the troubles started, Teddy Hodgson and Elton Knauf went via a backroad to a particular area to deliver much needed supplies and money to hospital workers in Lulungu. Part of the way there, they came across some rebels singing songs of rebellion, 'We want no words from the white man's God!" Although the missionaries tried to escape, they were forced to walk with the rebels. After a while the rebels stopped, raised machetes and hacked the two missionaries to pieces. It was a great shock to us all. All of our missionaries were fleeing from the Katanga province. We didn't find out for quite some time what had happened. It was hard to absorb what was happening when we were given the news as there was constantly bad news. It was a shock for us because Teddy was such a gentle man.

Due to the growing unrest in Congo, it was felt unwise for the Swedish school to be fully operational at Lemera. Ingemar Blom, the director of the school prepared to transfer school materials to Usumbura. At Baraka the situation was becoming more and more uncertain, and our missionaries decided to leave for Usumbura in Urundi. Their journey was hindered not only by military check points but by an earth tremor causing boulders to cover the road. Finally, they arrived at the border of Urundi and were welcomed into the Hollier's household.

Making Plans to Leave Due to the Continuing Unrest in Katanga Province.

Fighting broke out in Bukavu on 15 December 1960 and Congolese officials came up to Lemera on the 18th and advised closing the school two days early. Christmas passed without incident, and the new school term began again on 4 January 1961. We had 266 students on the register but only 59 arrived on that day. Students from Urundi were forbidden from entering the Congo. On 8 January, leaders of a political party were heading for the mission to demand the missionaries' houses and the telephone system which they thought was being used to communicate with Europe. The group were waylaid by the local Mwami (a local chief/king), who praised the work of the missionaries. It was at this time we knew we had to plan to leave. I can't say I can remember what I was feeling at the time.... these tense moments are hard to recall. We could only send letters if people were going out of the country to Burundi and so it became very difficult to make contact with home. The mission lorry was packed with suitcases, and we were preparing to travel but we needed travel permits. The military insisted that the lorry be taken to Uvira to be inspected and it was to be driven by the Congolese legal representative, Yohanna Ruhigita to be inspected. Yohanna set out for Uvira but by now his life was under threat. He was being accused of being a friend of the Europeans, helping them to leave with their belongings and embezzling the salaries of the teachers. Yohanna set out for Uvira, but God had other plans!

A short distance from the mission, a top-ranking official stopped the lorry and declared that they would never reach Uvira safely so ordered the lorry to be taken back to Lemera. When Yohanna arrived, he called out 'Mungu Yuko' – 'God exists!' He said that when he met the official it was like meeting his own father!

On 2 February 1961, the Swedish vice consul and Mr. Palmertz, the legal representative for the Swedish mission, arrived to talk over evacuation plans with the UN. All attempts to obtain fresh travel permits failed. On Monday 13 February, Patrice Lumumba's death was announced. He was a Congolese politician and independence leader who was leading the uprising in Leopoldville. At the same time no travel for 8 days was announced. In Bukavu, the situation began to change for the better. On Saturday 18 February

Petrus Gustavsson (a missionary from Bukavu) obtained a travel permit signed by the commander-in-chief of the army including an army escort, a sergeant and corporal, giving us permission to leave on the Sunday morning for Bukavu. We set out early and were stopped 12 times at gunpoint by the soldiers. The only way to cope with this ordeal was by holding my breath and praying! We arrived at noon. One hour after the arrival of our convoy, the commander who had signed the permit, was overthrown. We got there just in time!

Escape Across the Lake to Rwanda

Jim Liddle and I left for the UN headquarters that evening. The other missionaries stayed at the Swedish mission station. We left because we were not Swedish and so were not linked with any official consul. It was advised that we go to the UN in Bukavu. We were taken by army trucks to the lake side where a motor launch (these were small military vessels often used in Royal Navy service) was to take us across to Rwanda. Usually, the motor launch paddled mid-stream before setting the engines in motion to stop the soldiers getting ideas of movement on the lake and start shooting. That night as we left from the UN headquarters, the UN soldiers who were Nigerian at the time, put on a large party with loud drums to cover the sound of our motorboat escaping. That night God also provided a storm that covered the sound of the engines, so we were able to set the boat in motion straight away. We arrived in Shangugu (now Cyangugu), Rwanda, where we were hosted in a Belgian mission centre. The next morning missionaries from the Swedish mission took us up to their Swedish mission station in Shangugu. Later we were able to travel down to Usumbura (now Bujumbura). Jim Liddle left for England straight away and I left a week or so later in March of 1961.

Things had become so dangerous that we had to very quickly be moved out of the Congo and into Rwanda. Although some things would have been on the news back home, they did not receive the full picture. We had limited time to write letters during this time and so I was only able to write hurried notes to be sent back home.

You can see a telegram that was sent to my mum informing her of my upcoming return which I hoped to safely make.

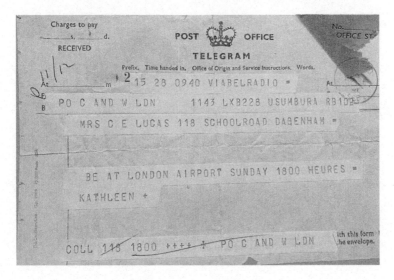

Telegram sent to my mum

On my return home, I began by saying 'Remember all the way, the Lord has led me.' I'd received a message from one of the prayer groups in Dagenham before I left home with a verse from Psalm 121: 7-8 *'The Lord will keep you from all harm. He will watch over your life; the Lord will watch over your coming and going both now and forevermore."* This

Feb 22. 1961.

Dear Mrs Lucas,

I have been thinking about you, and intending to write to you. We have all been very anxious about Kathleen and the other missionaries in the Congo, and we have been praying much for them. We got a letter last week-end from Mr Woodford telling us the latest news, that they were then still at Lemera but were safe, and they were doing all they could to get them safely out and home. I do trust you have good news soon. It has been and is a very difficult time for all of us with our dear ones out in Africa.

We must remember they are in our great Heavenly Father's care and keeping. And when Jesus said "Go ye into all the wor He said "Lo I am with you always." And ; ill never leave them, nor forsake them.

When I would worry about our girls I have to remind myself about these prom

A letter sent to my mum from Mrs Atkinson, Heather Rowlands mother, expressing concern for me.

verse meant so much more after all we had been through. I understood now why God had given me this verse to hold onto.

- -

Reflect…

Kathleen held onto a verse from God throughout all the difficulties she faced during the Congolese uprising. Can you think of a verse that has meant a lot to you in difficult times?

Has God ever provided a "storm" which you haven't understood at the time but later as you've reflected you've realised it was all part of His plan?

Chapter 6

Furlough and Return to the Congo

1962 - 1963

"The Lord is my shepherd, I lack nothing. He makes me lie down in green pastures, he leads me beside quiet waters, he refreshes my soul." Psalm 23:1-3

C oming home was challenging at this time as so much had changed back home. I was still suffering a great deal from the memories of all that had taken place. Although many people would have known some of what had happened in the Congo, no one really asked direct questions in those days. It was just not the way things were done. This was in the post war era where people lived with a 'stiff upper lip'.

Furlough

Normally when missionaries returned after a time abroad, they were invited by the churches that had supported them to a service to talk about God's work abroad and were given the opportunity to rebuild relationships and raise support for the next term of service on the mission field. I often felt that in these trips to other churches, I was telling of someone else's story rather than my own. People were often quite shocked that I wanted to go back! As so many Assemblies of God and Congo Evangelistic Mission missionaries arrived home at the same time, this presented a problem as there were insufficient churches to itinerate in and so we were encouraged to seek secular employment. After Easter, I was engaged as a teacher in William Ford School in Dagenham although I found this challenging after all I had been through on the mission field. I really was quite exhausted!

Ingegerd Rooth

Friendships from the mission field were hugely important to me as they were with people I had spent the past few years with as we had shared experiences of what we had been through. One such friend was Ingegerd Rooth who was a year and half older than me.

When I had previously travelled to Africa in 1958, I replaced Gunnel Molander who was on furlough. She returned in October 1960 but was transferred to a college in Urundi (now Burundi). In May 1961, I received a letter from my good friend, Ingegerd Rooth to say that Gunnel had been taken ill in Urundi and had passed away. The funeral had already taken place in Usumbura (now Bujumbura). Later Ingegerd wrote to me to recount what had happened to her in relation to a call she had had from Gunnel's parents.

"Six months after leaving Usumbura, the situation was calmer and I thought it was time to return to Africa, but a childhood dream of becoming a doctor would not leave me. I toyed with the idea of further studies but to train as a doctor would be costly and impossible for me. I was so frustrated until one Saturday morning in July 1961, I received a phone call from Gunnel Molander's parents. Her father began by saying, 'If you want to further your training, we are willing to help you get started.'

Even today, I have no idea that they knew I wanted to continue my training! Already a door had been opened. In fact it was not only a door but a highway to the future! This certainly was the Lord speaking to me. On Monday morning I lost no time. I took a train up to Stockholm where I signed up for courses in chemistry, physics and mathematics knowing that I would need this for my time in training as a doctor."

Not only did Ingrid complete her training as a doctor but she returned to the Congo where she worked tirelessly and then out to Tanganyika (now Tanzania) where she was working in the mosquito infested marsh land area of Mchukwi. Her research into malaria and a certain type of mosquito was honoured with a doctorate.

Ingegerd was a great friend. I owe her gratitude because she made my social life at Lemera a little more comfortable as she would do translation from Swedish into English. Before becoming a doctor Ingegerd was a midwife and nurse but still found the time to translate nearly the whole of Matthew's gospel into Kifulero, the local dialect. She also, with the help of the locals translated the whole of the New Testament chapter by chapter sending it to the Bible Society to be printed. At the time, they wanted one book to be sent out at a time, but due to the unrest she thought it better to send when and as she could. For many years Ingegerd would ring me every Christmas and Easter from Helsingborg in Sweden where she now lives but now with new technology we are able to FaceTime regularly! These lifelong relationships formed were so important to me.

A trip to see Rosalie Hegi in Switzerland

Rosalie Hegi, another great woman from the mission field, invited me to spend the New Year of 1962 with her in Switzerland. Once again, I was introduced to new customs but this time not so unlike our 'watch night' services at home. We went along to church in Langenthal giving thanks to God for His goodness over the past year and seeking His guidance, grace, and favour for the new year. After the service, the whole congregation were invited to a sumptuous meal together and the tables were well decorated with flowers and candles, and of course food! A day or two later we went to stay with some friends on their farm. It was bitterly cold and one night I was coughing violently. Suddenly Rosalie's friend came into the bedroom with a tablespoon of a dark mixture. She could not speak English and I could not speak German but all I needed to do was to open my mouth wide and swallow the medicine. Maybe it was the shock or the mixture, but I ceased coughing!

Return to Congo

I began preparing for my return to the Congo on 13th April 1962 to the shock of many. However, I knew I had to go as this was where God had called me to serve Him.

The situation there was much calmer, school had resumed at Lemera and I was invited to rejoin the staff. Back in London, the Oversees Missions' Council of AOG had written to say that John Burridge and Wesley Beardsmore were to come and evaluate the missions' stations at Baraka, Lulimba and Albertville (now Kalemie). They were already in Brussels processing their visas and they would then be able to take me up to Lemera. Knowing that I would need a travel visa to enter Congo I made an application via the Protestant Mission office in Brussels. This would mean a short stay in Brussels. I travelled from London on April 13th. The weather was fine, and I had a very pleasant journey.

At the airport I took a train to the centre of town and a taxi to Anderlecht where Albert Gunter and his wife were waiting for me. I had expected to meet John and Wesley there, but they had already returned to England because they had to wait for six weeks for their visas to come through. The people in the nursing home were pleased to see me again as many had remembered me from the days I was studying. Saturday morning, I went to inquire about my transit visa and was surprised to learn the office was closed.

On Monday morning I returned but the visa still had not been granted. They promised to phone the Gunters as soon as it was ready. True to their word we received a call to say that the visa was granted, and I could book a place on the plane for Usumbura (Bujumbura) on Friday.

The journey back to the Congo

I was extremely excited to be going back to the Congo after a year on furlough. It felt so natural. On Wednesday evening Eric, the high spirited 13-year-old younger son of the Gunters, was 'acting the goat' with a sheath knife. He accidently flicked it and caught my arm. A doctor in the congregation attended to me and managed to apply two stitches on my arm and gave me penicillin capsules. That saved me a trip to the hospital. Despite that, my journey to Congo continued. I still bear the scar!

At London airport, the officials were strict when weighing my luggage. I was limited to 20 kilograms. John and Wesley had offered to take my books so that they were not added to the weight of my luggage but at Brussels airport no questions were asked! My luggage went through without any problem!

Ingrid Kymell & I outside the church building

Ingrid Kymell had joined the staff on a year's contract and was enjoying her time both at the school and out in the villages wherever possible. She was already there when I got back. In January 1962, when she joined, we shared accommodation which seemed to leave some students amused whenever they saw us together because Ingrid was extremely tall in contrast to my 4ft10inches!

The refugee situation was steadily getting worse. The Red Cross teams were very active in the region. We often relied upon them to bring supplies from Usumbura or to take our mail into town.

On arrival back to the Congo, the rains had been heavy for quite a few weeks and the well-known single lane mountain tracks presented a hazardous journey - I was now finally back in Lemera!

Now they were repairing bridges that had been broken for a while. Ingrid had bought a car from some friends going home on furlough and I had heard that my unaccompanied luggage was at the customs office in Usumbura. We travelled there to retrieve it. My passport was in Leopoldville (now Kinshasa) at this time for yet another visa but fortunately for me I was only asked for my identity card at the border and customs control. We had been warned by the other missionaries that we could only take a small amount in the car back with us up to the value of a thousand francs which was about £30 or $40. When we got to the custom's building the official asked, 'What have you got in that trunk?' I tried to appear unconcerned and said, 'I've just retrieved my luggage at customs control and here is the permit.' To my relief he just said 'ok, have a good journey!' I was quite concerned they could have taken a lot of money from us, but God knew what I needed and had gone ahead of us! The contents of my luggage were going to have to last me for up to 5 years on the field, so I certainly did not want any of it taken away!

At the end of July, we were asked by the state to be examiners at the central jury which was giving students from unrecognised schools the opportunity to receive a state recognised diploma. After this had been sorted, Ingrid and I left for East Africa for a holiday.

Holidaying in East Africa in a VW Beetle
For our holiday I guess we just figured we had a car and all we needed to do was to get going! Not long after the start of our journey we were reduced to crawling along the road as there was a problem with the car. Eventually we saw a sign 'Williamson and Diamonds Limited Garage'. With a sigh of relief, we pulled in. The African in charge spoke excellent English, looked at our VW and said, 'I am well able to deal with the problem, but I only have shock absorbers suitable for Landrovers.' He told us to sit in the camp while he sent for spares. A cyclist went off to get them! As we waited another African came and offered us tea which was well received. A couple of hours later he came again and apologised for the long wait and offered us a meal. There in

the middle of nowhere we sat eating steak, chips, cabbage and carrots, followed by fresh fruit. A luxury hotel service in the middle of nowhere! Finally, suitable shock absorbers arrived, were fitted and we were on our way to Dodoma, in Tanzania.

Our travels began in Urundi. From Usumbura, we travelled to the missions' stations of Mugara, Kilemba and Kitega. We then went into Tanganyika (Tanzania) where we stayed with Church Missionary Society missionaries from Uganda. Staying at various mission stations was certainly a cheaper way of doing holidays. People from other mission stations often did this to us too, coming to stay with us in the Congo. Our travel across Tanganyika was across rough roads which had a devastating effect on the shock absorbers in our beetle. What on earth gave us the idea we could travel in a Volkswagen Beetle around Africa?

In Tanzania, we continued to Dar es Salaam and later into neighbouring Kenya, where we enjoyed a day in the national park! It was there that we saw lions hunting their prey quite close to the car. We saw many giraffes, ostriches and monkeys everywhere. Our next stop was Kisumu, in western Kenya and then we drove to Kampala in Uganda. Throughout the whole journey we only really saw lorries on the road and there we were in our VW Beetle! We finally made our way to Rwanda and across the border into the Congo. We were on the road for about two months and arrived back to the Congo in time for the new school year to begin.

There were many adventures on the holiday around East Africa. One that particularly comes to mind was when we got to the border of one of the countries ready to cross but only to discover we could not because of a local border curfew. We found ourselves in the middle of nowhere, not knowing what to do. We asked the police what to do and they replied that they did not know! In the end we asked if we could sleep in the police station on the floor as we had all our camping supplies with us. Ingrid really was an adventurous one and I think she was glad to have someone to adventure with her and I was that person!

The New School Term Begins

We arrived in time for the new school term to begin in September. At the start of the new school year the number of students in each class was extremely high and so we desperately needed more staff. The director was a Norwegian missionary, Odd Boresan. He asked me if I knew of any French speaking teachers who could come and join us. Remembering that the IBTI (International Bible Training Institute in Burgess Hill, West Sussex) often had students from abroad, I wrote to ask them if they could help us. A lady from Switzerland called Madeleine Zbinden happened to be at the IBTI at that time as she had just left her teaching post in Lausanne to spend some time with her brother Jean-Jacquess Zbinden, who lived there. The reason she had left her teaching post was something of a mystery, but she was at the IBTI at the time. A former IBTI student had recently been there and had spoken about her work in the Congo prior to independence. She had mentioned the need for French speaking teachers, especially in a college located near Bukavu. The former student happened to have been a Swedish missionary at the nursery and primary school in Lemera. When my letter arrived Jean-Jacques ran up to Madeleine and said, 'Read this!' They realised both appeals were being made from the same source. I had spoken only about Lemera in South Kivu province whereas the Swede had spoken of a college near Bukavu. Both were talking of the same place. Madeleine prayed and realised it was the will of God for her to come and join us as she was a French speaking teacher out of work at the time. She contacted UNESCO. At the time, the UN were paying teachers to come and rebuild the Congo and they often reached out to missionaries. She was due to arrive in February which once again was another amazing coincidence, or rather a God appointed moment!

A visit from the UN

In December we had a surprise visit from a large number of Swedish and Norwegian soldiers who were working with the United Nations. They were based in Kamina in Katanga province, but they had not left camp since they arrived in Congo. At the time Moise Tshombe was in control (he had replaced Patrice Lumumba). He considered the UN the number one enemy so would not let them out. There were not only soldiers there, but also a pilot and a plane. They came up to Lemera in UN lorries. They were fascinated by the scenery and immediately cameras began to flash all over the station. They said they had never seen such scenery as the Lemera mountains. Naturally they were served coffee and cake before returning to Bukavu. Later, during their return flight back to Kamina their planes circled Lemera twice causing quite a stir amongst the local population who thought the sky was falling in. They had never seen a plane so low before. Ingrid left for Sweden shortly afterward in the January of 1962.

My mum had given me her Christmas pudding recipe, so I decided to make this for us at Christmas. I followed the recipe as closely as possible. I had carefully gathered some fruit from Tanganyika (Tanzania) and found other fruits to make up the weight. I remember sitting up until midnight waiting for the stove to cook the Christmas pudding. It was well worth the effort and my guests made sure nothing was left over. I was determined to make sure that this Christmas I would have Christmas pudding and cake! For me, Christmas pudding was so important as the Swedish had so many of their own traditions that I wanted to share some of our traditions from home.

Shortly after the New Year I had a bad bout of tonsillitis and was in bed for a fortnight. I reacted badly to the penicillin treatment and other antibiotics were prescribed. At this time, I received a card from Albert Gunter and his wife back in Belgium. It was posted in November to say that Eric, the younger son who had accidentally injured me, had passed away. Apparently, he had experienced an epileptic fit and failed to recover. It was deeply saddening news to receive.

Madeleine had arrived and was adapting well to life in Lemera. We now had a generator that was restored so we had electricity every evening for four hours from 6pm. It was such a relief not to walk from room to room with a storm lantern. On my last trip to town, I had even bought two hot plates for cooking our evening meal, but I still had to use the primus stove during the day.

In May, the government announced that certain teachers would be offered a free ticket home to Europe for the summer and the names of those who had qualified would be announced on the national radio. Each evening we waited for the news bulletin. On June 17th, my name was announced! My flight would leave for Usumbura (now Bujumbura) on June 28th and was to return in August via Leopoldville (now Kinshasa). The Oversees Missions Council of AOG had written to say that Makombo, Lulimbo and Albertville stations were functioning and the school in Lulimba would be ready in late August. They asked me to direct the school there. David Pike had already been appointed to take my place in Lemera.

I do not remember a lot about my time home but it was filled with visiting friends and local churches, and buying anything I needed to take back with me. My holiday in Europe was soon over and the evening before I returned to Africa, I attended a prayer meeting at my home church, Bethel in Dagenham where there was a message in tongues followed by the interpretation which said, 'No matter what they do to you, trust in the Lord.' Little did I know how much I would need to hang on to these words in the future.

Reflect...

When Kathleen returned home after having to escape from Congo it was not normal in those days to process through trauma but to have a 'stiff upper lip'. When it comes to pain and difficulty in your own life and ministry, do you tend to bury it or talk about it? How could you ensure you process pain well?

Kathleen's two-month holiday around East Africa in the VW beetle was obviously very enjoyable and refreshing for her. How are you ensuring in your ministry life that you take good rest and do things which "fill your tank"?

Who refreshes your soul?

From Dagenham To Africa with love

Chapter 7

House Arrest & Escape

1964

"When you pass through the waters, I will be with you; and when you pass through the rivers, they will not sweep over you. When you walk through the fire, you will not be burned; the flames will not set you ablaze. For I am the Lord your God, the Holy One of Israel, your Saviour."
Isaiah 43:2-3

Conditions in the Congo were stabilising, and work had restarted on three of our mission stations. Earlier in 1962, the British Assemblies of God had invited two Congolese men to come to its General Conference to present the prepared projects regarding the Bible School, training of medical staff and the building of a secondary school. Pastor Eliyah Yuma, the well-respected elected leader of UPM GBI (Union of Pentecostal Missionaries of Great Britain and Northern Ireland) and Jean Sulemani, a Lemera graduate were the chosen representatives. Their visit was very inspiring. Eliyah's keen sense of humour and humble walk with God stirred the Women's Missionary Auxiliary organisation to pray and support the projects with financial and practical help wherever possible.

Eliyah Yuma and Jean Sulemani visit the Assemblies of God conference

My short visit home ended, and my return flight was booked for 7 August via Leopoldville. This was my first visit to the bustling capital. Being the dry season, everything was covered in a thick layer of dust and the heat was stifling. For two or three days I was back and forth to the Air Sabena offices regarding the last lap of my journey. Finally, word came through that my flight was confirmed for August 11th. Friends were at the airport to meet me, and Wesley Beardsmore took me up to Lemera to collect some of my belongings in preparation for work in Lulimba. Before independence, the journey to Lulimba would have been via Uvira and Baraka but we were advised to avoid Baraka due to conflict. This meant a three-day journey via Mwenga. The roads were in a terrible state of disrepair and in many places, we were travelling at a snail's pace of 2km an hour! We were glad for the Land Rover. My first few days at Lulimba left me trying to get the dust from the road out of my clothes and nostrils!

Building Work and Snakes!
During the dry season, water had to be collected from the nearest river almost a kilometre away. For domestic use, we needed to boil it for 20 minutes and then filter it, so we rationed our water.

I began to prepare for the school intake and rather than administer an entrance exam, I decided to accept the 56 students who had been selected by the primary schools of the region. They were all aged 11+ and I would give them an exam after 6 weeks of learning instead. I thought this would be fairer as I did not know what they had been taught. At the end of the class exam, I would remain with 35 students in the class.

The lack of cement and other materials in Albertville (now Kalemie) meant that the school building was not yet complete. No doors. No windows. The floor was uncemented. During the first few lessons, many villagers stood in the doorway and others blocked the window to get a glimpse of secondary school life. Early in November cement finally arrived. Wesley and the builders did all they could to produce bricks. The mixture of one part cement and 20 parts dry earth was fed into the brick press. And then they were left in the sun to become bone dry or in some cases left on the church floor as a precaution. Unfortunately, work had just started when it poured with rain ruining the one and half bags of cement we had. I had been at Lulimba for several weeks and it was suggested that we travel to Fizi to register my arrival in the county offices.

Wesley and Hannah Beardsmore and I set off at 7.15am. We reached Fizi at 11am only to find that no one had come to work that day! The whole journey was over rough escarpment roads. Fortunately, on the way back we were able to buy some tomatoes which were the only fresh vegetables we had been able to buy for weeks.

We heard that flights between Albertville and Bukavu were becoming more frequent so when I was invited to Lemera for Christmas, I was able to book a flight for the 23rd of December. Friends took me up to Lemera on Christmas Eve to rejoin Madeleine Zbinden for the celebrations. It was only five months since I had left Lemera, yet it was surprising to see how many new people had joined the staff. How grateful I was to be back home and to be refreshed by the cool mountain air.

The flight back to Albertville was most interesting. I was able to recognise Uvira and Baraka mission stations and Usumbura airport. Back in Albertville, I was able to obtain books to cover the new curriculum at the education office, not just for the present school year but for the whole of the three years of 'Cycle d'orientation' which was the three-year preparatory course. The class at Lulimba was now reduced and so made my task a little easier.

Rains had been relentless and so the water drums were overflowing. But there was a rather negative side to this, snakes became more active. There was a snake in the classroom one day as I was about to enter with a couple of boys. I knew there was nothing they could grab hold of. I saw a stick and threw it in to kill the snake. Another time there was a Black Mamba on the veranda of the big house where I lived. There was another huge green snake that disappeared in the wood planks into the building site. The rains had clearly disturbed them. You always needed a quick reaction to deal with them. Whether scared or not you just had to do something whether that be run or find the nearest implement to you and hit it on the head. We were told hit its head, not its middle.

February 1964

Early February found me back in Albertville again. I had a minor operation to remove a lump from my breast. The doctor sent a biopsy to the lab in Leopoldville and said the results would be back in a month's time. In March, the doctor announced the good news that there was no sign of malignancy but a filament that needed to be cleansed. The doctor was surprised and glad at the report. I had medication and injections to help. The wound had to heal naturally for when the stitches were removed it bled so much that the cavity needed to be plugged. Eventually, it healed. It had been a major cause of worry for my parents back home, more so due to postal service delays which meant they had to wait longer to find out the good news. It would have taken between three and four weeks before I could post a letter in the town which was four hours away. We were totally dependent on people passing through to post our letters for us. Of course, there were no telephones in those days.

The Beardsmore family who had travelled to Rhodesia to bring their sons home for the Christmas holiday, were back at the mission station. That was around the end of February. They had been somewhat delayed as Hannah, Wesley's wife, had been taken ill and needed hospital treatment.

Now fully recovered Hannah, who was a nurse, had opened the dispensary and was receiving on average 50 to 60 patients a day! My class at present was housed in a maternity ward at the dispensary because unfortunately the rains had demolished a great deal of the school building. The food situations in Albertville lacked variety and so we were still unable to get tinned vegetables, but the UN were being withdrawn from Albertville at the beginning of April and so we received large tins of beans, peas, tomatoes, dried onions, dried milk, butter fat, peaches and apples and canned chicken - a whole young chicken in a tin! What a rich blessing as we had only been able to get tinned sardines previously.

April 1964

In April, UPM GBI, held a conference to discuss future projects and the AOG Oversees Missions' Council was represented by members of the council, Pastors John Carter and Walter Hawkins. Rumours of growing unrest in the country were causing concern but throughout the conference the pastors reassured the oversees mission delegation that it was political due to the upcoming elections and not anti-European. They said we had no need to worry. During the conference it was suggested that the big house at Lulimba be converted into two apartments to accommodate the Evans family who were to join us from Albertville.

Imagine our amusement when young Ralf Beardsmore came into the kitchen as we were trying to prepare a meal and asked, 'Dad, can I play the record, 'there's no place like home!'

25th May 1964

On Monday, May 25th Geoff Hawksley insisted on having a letter of introduction to show at every barrier he may encounter on the journey. He made it safely home, but shortly after he left us a pastor came up to warn that soldiers were fleeing the rebel troops. He advised us to put food and petrol out of site. We were informed that they may commandeer our food or even the vehicles. We worked until early morning putting food and school supplies in the loft. Next day we buried drums of petrol in the outside dropped toilets. The local people would never go into our toilet area and so wouldn't have ever found the petrol. As an aside, all our toilets were outside and when we needed to go and relieve ourselves, we would tap on the tin door and wait for the cockroaches to run down the toilet. We didn't want to see them so gave them time to disappear!

Context to the Political and Social Situation in Congo

At this point, I feel it would be helpful to give you some context to the political and social situation in the Congo. In his book 'Congo Saga - an authentic record of the heroes of the cross during the Simba rising' David W Truby gives a good understanding about what had brought the country to this point. He says, *'Up to the latter part of the eighteenth century, the interior of Africa was largely unknown and unexplored. Livingstone and Stanley penetrated into the heart of this continent between the years 1874 and 1877 and in the subsequent scramble for Africa, King Leopold of Belgium took over Congo as his private estate. In 1885 it became Congo Free State, and Belgium began to administer it as a colony in 1908, but when Stanley arrived, he found that other white men had preceded him.*

For almost fifty years Arab slave traders and merchants seeking both gold and ivory had penetrated far into Congo, pillaging, raiding, and massacring all who tried to resist them in their quest for spoils of white ivory, pure gold and black life. Fear and tyranny reigned among the primitive peoples of Congo through the unscrupulous Arab Chief, Hammed Ben-Mohammed, more commonly known as Tippo Tip. On one occasion Livingstone testified that he saw slave traders shoot into a crowd killing and wounding men, women and children.....it was not until September 22nd, 1894 that the last Arab bastion capitulated at Pweto (in the state now known as Katanga) and the Congolese were rid of the evil inflicted upon them.

Then followed 70 years of Belgian colonial rule....they ruled with a firm hand, built cities, cultivated plantations, constructed roadways, railways, bridges.....they provided educational, medical and social services....but as the years passed by many Congolese began to envy the superior position of their colonisers and longed for the day when the country would be independent and they would retain their own profits and be free from the yoke of white rule. Many traders had been indiscreet, unfair and had taken advantage of the situation. In the early years many had exploited the Congolese for rubber and atrocities had been committed. Very little reward was given for hard labour and the molesting of Congolese women was not unknown. In the late 1950's the number of educated Congolese had increased rapidly and pressure for independence became more pronounced...'[2].

Unrest

Some of the rebels fighting were very well educated but just misguided in their sense of wanting to be independent. From 1948 to 1958 the Congolese were given preparation time before independence from Belgian rule and then two years to change over government, but it did not all fall into place as anticipated. The national army still had Belgian commanders teaching the new troops. Some people were in uproar at this and so rebel groups were created who wanted to fight on their own. Moise Tshombe who was in power in Katanga, endeavoured to break away from central government and form an independently ruled province. He was heavily influenced by Chinese communistic thinking. The UN forces intervened and crushed the uprising, banishing Tshombe. Three other Prime Ministers followed but all were unsuccessful, and the Congo became hugely unstable. As a result of the unrest, groups formed causing local disturbances and revolts broke out against local authorities. Rebel groups were formed gaining more and more power. Tshombe was invited back to try to bring stability to the country but his requests for reconciliation were ignored and eventually a full-scale rebellion broke out all over the Congo. This is the political situation we were living in at the time.

---

[2] 1965. David W Truby. Congo Saga

The rebels known as 'Mulelistes,' were followers of Mulele, a Congolese leader who was convinced that communism was the way to power and freedom. Believing that the government had sold the country to the Americans and imperialists, many well educated Congolese joined forces with him. He also recruited young boys in a youth movement called 'Jeunesse'. They were boy(child) soldiers. Sadly, the Muleliste were heavily influenced by witchcraft, superstition, cannibalism, and drugs. Some drank a concoction of animal blood, mixed with herbs and leaves believing that this magic would protect them from harm. Some of them would smear themselves with the magic concoction too. They had greetings between each other. In the daytime it was 'Maji Ya Mulele' meaning 'water of Mulele' (magic water with power) or 'Maji ya milele' meaning 'water of eternal life'. In the area we were in, in eastern Africa the language used was known as pure Swahili. 'Maji ye milele' did mean eternal life but it was also connected to magic. At night the greeting was 'Simba' meaning 'lion'. The rebels we encountered were called either 'Mileliste' or 'Simba.'

28th April 1964
Thursday evening, as we were having our meal, all the missionaries from Mokombo arrived.

They had been advised by their pastor to take a holiday in Tanganyika. They planned to continue through to Albertville the next day but one of the pastors came up to say rebel troops were in the vicinity, and it would be best to wait before any further travel.

We hoped the rebels would pass through the area and just carry on. It would be safer to wait till Saturday for the missionaries to move on. We said we would join them, but on Saturday morning at 6am we were awakened by several troops dressed in an unusual assortment of clothing, branches and feathers in their hats, some wearing grass skirts, some with automatic weapons, some with bows and arrows or bush knives. They asked for the keys to Wesley Beardsmore's Landrover and a radio transmitter. We had not yet received our radio transmitters that had been ordered some weeks earlier, so we replied that there were none on the station. They repeatedly asked for the keys for the Land Rover. By this time one of the local pastors had arrived to try to intervene but a rifle was put to his head with a finger on the trigger. The keys to the Land Rover were handed over and that was the first of our vehicles to leave the station.

The events that took place at Lulimba following our 129 days in confinement reveal the gracious protection, provision, and prophetic encouragement from the Lord. For instance, the doctor treating Hannah Beardsmore over Christmas was also from Derbyshire. He was keenly interested in the work Hannah was doing in the dispensary and maternity unit at Lulimba. This led to contacts with the Rhodesian (now Zimbabwe) Red Cross, resulting in a gift of medicine to the value of £100. These medicines proved most helpful to pacify the sick and wounded 'Muleliste' or

'Simba.' Rebels. They of course had their own concoctions or remedies, superstitions, and magic powers but when all else failed they were glad of Hannah's help.

God's Provision

In April, Geoff Hawksley and Wesley Beardsmore were in Albertville (now Kalemie) seeking building material when they were recognised by a local tradesman, working at the time for the UN. He asked them if they would accept what he had in the jeep as the UN were withdrawing their activities. Immediately, they filled the Land Rover and truck hence all three mission stations had a supply or a certain quantity of food during that challenging time.

1st June 1964

Another group of rebels arrived at the house dressed and armed like our earlier visitors. They had a letter from the leader thanking us for the loan of the first Land Rover but now they needed a second which would be returned within a month. Once again, the pastors tried to intervene but when a gun was raised the keys were given over. There was a most unpleasant moment when they had difficulty starting the engine but when it began to start, they were soon off at full speed with Cyril Cross's Land Rover. From then on, each day, 5-year-old Margaret Cross prayed that 'Tembo' (the Swahili name for 'elephant' which had been the name given by Margaret to the Land Rover) would be returned.

10th June 1964

Ten days later we were awakened at 3am by a noisy threatening group of men, who earlier had been workers at the mission but sadly they abandoned the work to join forces with the Mulelistes. They came for the remaining Landrover with a promise to return it to us the next morning. That was the last we saw of it. Nothing was taken from the hands of a civilian, so when they inspected our identity cards they had to be put on the floor and they would pick them up to look at them.

A big barricade was formed around the mission station which meant we could no longer safely leave but were confined to an area decided by the rebels. People from the surrounding area would come to bring staple food like potatoes or rice for us but they would be confronted by the Simbas and made to leave the food on the floor often being beaten. The Simbas would not take the food from the hands of the people and especially not from a woman as they believed it would contaminate their magic powers.

22nd June 1964

I was informed that there was to be a school inspection. We were still running the school at the time partly because it gave us something to do whilst contained. The building work had come to a stop as the builders had run away. I had about 25 students at this time who were from the village. Many of the local people, especially the younger ones had been recruited to be part of the Muleliste. The local area was made up of tribes of about five to seven clans and the area of Baraka was represented by a number of different clans. Three of these had opened the door wide for rebels and they were extremely anti-white. The Wabembe people were strong followers of Mulele and so the national army were trying to get rid of them. The Wabembe used to flee unless they felt they could fight and win.

On the day of the inspection, one of the boys begged me, 'Please, can I leave?' I asked why and his reason was that a member of his family was sought by the rebels. He was blacklisted and if that member was not found, the rest of the family would be killed. At that time, if you were a friend of Europeans, you were then in a difficult position and had to flee. At the end of the school session, the inspector arrived. He was a Muleliste rebel leader, and he gave an elaborate speech emphasising that the revolution was for their own good and that as soon as they had control of the country they would subsidise everything we needed to complete the school building and that materials would be overflowing. When he left, the students said that I had gained a 'victory'! I asked why and they replied, 'Well, the Muleliste should not even be in the same room as a woman!' All my students were between the ages of 14 and 25 and were eyed by the rebels to be boy soldiers. This was the real reason the 'inspector' had come up - to scout them out! They gave speeches like this in all the schools trying to recruit young men to their cause.

The rebels came up to the house almost daily asking for food or just helping themselves to what they wanted. Eliya

Yuma came to live at Lulimba to encourage the local pastors and Christians. We, the missionaries, listened to radio news bulletins regularly - especially the BBC which was being relayed from Dar es Salaam, the Swedish radio and radio Burundi. One evening we were listening to the Swedish radio, and we learnt that Naomi Liddle's father who was Swedish had passed away.

We heard that all the missionaries in Lemera had been led to safety by Marandure, who years earlier, had been teaching in a mission school and knew Johanna Ruhigita who had helped me out previously. The news bulletins informed us of all the effort being made to help us. The Swedish missionaries in Kigoma, Tanganyika invited us to attend a mission conference to help us get out. The Bjorndins, the Swedish missionaries helping us, received our reply to their invitation. They were encouraged and tried to send some money together with little food parcels over to us. They also said they would send our mail from Tanganyika home and would keep any mail for us, so we used their postal address.

25th June 1964
This letter was written to my parents at the time from the Oversees Missions' Department of Assemblies of God to update them on the situation:

Dear Mr. and Mrs. Lucas,

I am writing to assure you that we are very conscious of your anxiety at this time and that we are doing all we possibly can to obtain news of your loved one for you.

Owing to the breakdown in the usual means of communication with our missionaries we are in the position of not knowing their present welfare. The tension caused by the lack of news is aggravated by the reports of political unrest in the Kivu district and by many rumours in this country. May I ask for your own sake you ignore the rumours and statements which appear in the press. This week we have investigated many rumours, and all have proved to be untrue.

We have made arrangements with the Foreign Office for an aircraft to fly from Usumbura to Lulimba and Makombo in an attempt to establish contact with our missionaries at these places. The Consul at Elisabethville is in contact with the Congolese Army Commander who is trying to gain news of our missionaries in Albertville. Immediately this information is available it will be passed by cable to the Foreign Office and by phone to us. We shall let you know immediately we have any news for you.

We are praying especially for you. May our Lord grant His peace and blessing, Yours very sincerely,

G.M.SWIFT.

Any messages and gifts that came to us were conveyed across the lake by canoe, by African Christians via Lwata or Baraka. They risked their lives doing so since there was a curfew between 6pm and 6am. Likewise, Christians in Usumbura (now Bujumbura), Burundi were doing the same. Some may have been our Christian friends who had gone there to flee. They were smuggling packages up to us during this time.

18th August 1964

A letter was sent to the Oversees Mission Council in London via the Bjordins, which said:

"We are planning to come over to you for the conference to which you have invited us. Anything you can do for us will be appreciated. Please look after any letters which may come to you for us."

That was written by Cyril Cross to the Bjordins. The Bjordins continued to say to the office in London, "Aren't these letters worth more than gold and jewels? We just cried when we got them. We shall try to keep in contact with that person."

They could not dare go to the mission as they might have been recognised and would have been in danger. The letter went on to say, "It seems they have received the food we sent because they answer a question, we ask in a few lines that we wrote within the tin box. We have continued to send messages every week with a little money. It is not much but enough to pay for a postage stamp and should we need it, to pay for a runner to go and ask for help! We continue to send messages every week. We have no idea what is getting there and what isn't."

It was very dangerous particularly for those bringing us messages and I will forever be grateful for those who risked their lives to make contact with us.

20th August 1964

We heard that Gaston Soumialot, the leader in the Stanleyville (now Kisangani) troubles, had come to Lulimba headquarters travelling with a whole entourage of rebels. He had a journalist with him and whoever he was, had written us a letter saying he was willing to conduct us out via a northern route through Baraka. When we heard that Soumialot had come, we asked to see him.

We of course sent a letter first to request this. Surprisingly, he agreed for us to meet him! Four of us went along to the headquarters. We waited for a while, expecting to be ushered into another room to speak to this important official. Little did we know that the dishevelled man, slumped in a chair in front of us, wearing a cap was Soumialot himself. It seemed as though he was doped or had drunk all his medicine, but the men working with him were smart and one of them was the journalist. When they knew we all wanted to go to the conference they refused saying that only the men could go because women do not go to conferences. Then he read the letter asking for a travel permit and the reason given was that we were a little stressed! The journalist was angry when he read that. He said: 'If the world outside hears of this it would make pages and pages of news and our revolution will be reported falsely.' That put an end to that visit. We had hoped this would be our escape, but it was not to be at this time. We went back to the house empty handed.

23rd August 1964

I mentioned before that Margaret Cross, the five-year-old, prayed daily for her father's Landrover to be returned. Her prayer was answered on 23 August when Johanna, a local former Christian, now a captain in the rebel army, returned the vehicle. Prior to being taken, it had hardly done two years and was in excellent condition. But when it was returned, it was in a sorry state. The back door had been wrenched off and the shock absorbers plus the welding attaching them to the axels had broken away completely. The engine was in poor condition and a plug of wood substituted for a carburettor. The gear box was ruined and only the front wheel drive could be used. This was the only vehicle returned to us. Ironically having assessed the damage, the men set about to repair what they could for us. We still had one other vehicle which belonged to Audrey Brereton. It was untouched because it belonged to a woman!

In some ways I was shielded as I kept myself busy in the most difficult times with teaching school and trying to keep it going. I also spent time teaching little Margaret. The rebels would often come and standby. In the end I called them our feathered friends to make things less difficult especially for Margaret. This changed to calling them 'FF' in case the rebels spoke English and got angry at what I was saying.

4th September 1964

The local population were getting very anxious for the national army had threatened to kill all the Wabembe people because they had opened the door wide for the rebels in the first place. At that point a lot of our local Christians had fled into the bush and built grass huts to hide in.

8th September 1964

A heavily armed group of rebels burst into the mission station. They posted guards around the houses. They went into the house and marched the Hawksley's and the Cross family up to the big house, but they kept Audrey Brereton by herself alone in the small house. At gunpoint they repeatedly asked her if she was afraid to die. She found herself saying in Swahili 'Mungu Anajua' meaning 'God knows'. Then the rebel soldier asked her, 'do you want to die?' She replied, 'Sitaki Kufa' meaning 'I don't want to die.' He was very aggressive during this time and asked questions repeatedly. He lowered the gun and stormed up to the big house. In a raging temper, he separated the women from the men. The men were kept in one room and we women were lined up in a corridor while he ran up and down next to us with a rifle. He repeatedly asked us questions about petrol wanting to know where it had been hidden. We knew where it was of course, but we had decided to say, 'That's the affair of the men, they have the dealings with the car.' The soldier marched continually up and down the corridor with his rifle over his shoulder. Suddenly, Margaret Cross who was standing between me and her mother, cried out 'Mummy, is he going to shoot us?' Immediately I was prompted to reply, 'Margaret, he'll not touch us.'

He sent Naomi to the Liddle's bedroom with a guard and then he took me into my room. I was asked if I was willing to work in Congo? I replied that I was willing to work for the Lord in Congo. This annoyed him. He then suggested I might like to make a present for his wife, looking at the sewing machine. I told him she could have a dress that I saw in the room, but he told me it was too small for his wife. He then went out and left a young man with a bush knife on guard in the room with me. I could hear that he called for Jim Liddle and asked for his radio. He then came back to me and asked for the present for his wife, so I picked up the dress to give to him and he said that its presentation was not good enough as a present for his wife. He told me to wrap it up, which I proceeded to do. He laid it to one side and then suddenly, his mood changed. He left the room and called for all the soldiers to leave. They had come in like roaring lions and left like sheep! They'd been with us for more than an hour and a half. All this time, Eliya Uma and a group of Christians were praying for our safety. They had been unable to come up to the house, but they stood under the trees near the church seeking God on our behalf. The Lord had heard and answered their prayers.

When Albertville (now Kalemie) was retaken by Katangese national army troops, the rebels became more threatening because they heard rumours of what was happening, and they were continuing to try to re-take other places. Then Bendera, a hydroelectric plant area, just 45 miles from us was retaken and so the Muleliste fled passing through Lulimba on their way to Fizi.

It was later that day, when Barbara asked me how I could be so confident in replying to Margaret that we would not come to harm. I told her of the prayer meeting the night before I came back to the Congo as hands were being laid on me and people prayed for me, that the message in tongues was given and the interpretation was 'no matter what they do unto you, trust in the Lord.' I said to Barbara that this was the message, and I was confident it was for that moment. All year I had been wondering what it was for. Was it that I was going to Lulimba where Wesley Beardsmore and John Burridge had earlier a couple of years before been threatened by the Jeunesse or was it trouble with students or was it the operation I had had? None of that seemed to be relevant but this was certainly the moment. I remember saying 'The worst is over! Nothing we go through now will be as bad as this.' All year, God had been preparing me for that moment.

10th September 1964
A few days later, Eliya Uma came to say that he would be leaving to go into hiding. He was blacklisted for being accused of being a friend of Europeans and helping them

and because he had visited Europe. We continued to be troubled by the rebels daily for almost another month.

4th October 1964

On Sunday, 4th October, we went to church in the morning, but attendance was very poor. Most of the villagers had left for their own hideouts in the mountain. Pastor Joshua read Romans 13:1-7, emphasising that God had placed governments in place to bring rule into the situation. At 1.45pm, we heard gunshots from the government troops who had reached Lulimba. They were clearing the area systematically of anyone who was against them. Every house was searched for rebels and then set alight. We could see the progress from the smoke rising. It took a while for them to reach the mission. At 3pm, they came up to the house and they gave us an hour to be ready to leave.

A convoy was formed in Lulimba village. An armoured vehicle was in the lead, followed by six armoured trucks with national troops. Then, Audrey Brereton's Volkswagen with the Liddle family, Cyril's crippled Landrover with Barbara, Margaret and myself with Cyril driving. The other missionaries were in army vehicles. The group set off with guns firing all the time. At a certain point, we were stopped whilst the soldiers cleared an area where earlier that day they had petrol bombs thrown at them. They wanted to ensure it was clear for us to go through. We reached Bendera at 9pm. Bendera was a model village built to house Europeans during the construction of the hydroelectric plant which supplied Albertville with electricity. The African director placed the best two houses at our disposal for the night. As we entered the house, Margaret was saying 'Thank you Jesus, thank you Jesus for giving us Tembo back'.

5th October 1964

At 8am the next morning we set off for Albertville with military escort. Colonel Kakudji welcomed us at his headquarters, and we were invited to prepare ourselves a meal from his well-stocked larder. Later that day, we were taken to the hotel in town. The manager and his wife were delighted to see us. They had seen our Landrovers being used by the rebels and feared the worst. Places were booked on flights for Wednesday and Thursday to Usumbura, Burundi on small seven-seater planes. We often took boats across the lake, but these had all stopped because of rebel activity. We were welcomed by Mr and Mrs Johnson, missionaries in Usumbura who accommodated us in their mission guest house.

Interestingly we had formally been encouraged by the journalist mentioned earlier to escape up through Baraka but decided against this. Looking back, it was a wise decision as if we had gone through the north we would have seen the horrific devastation left behind by the rebels which would have been quite traumatic. What had been done to so many was unthinkable!

13th October 1964

Walter Hawkins, who was overseeing the OMC for AOG arrived for a debriefing session on 13th October from the

UK to discuss our future. When Walter arrived, he told us that a week of prayer had been held for our safety across all the AOG churches in the UK and that the week of prayer ended on the 3rd of October, and we were rescued on the 4th of October - what an incredible answer to prayer!

During the debriefing, future work for missionaries was discussed. I asked to go back to Bukavu to help in the school that had been evacuated there from Lemera. They simply responded to me, 'be prepared'. I thought 'be prepared for what?' Things seemed to have got better back in the Congo.

When Walter Hawkins arrived for the debriefing, he wanted to discuss future appointments. We were told to take a rest, but the question was where? If we came home, we would have to go on itineraries around churches, speaking and sharing about what we had been through. Certainly that would not have been a rest for us. I was told that I could go back to Bukavu to take a rest with Swedish friends there and to consult the Norwegian Pentecostal doctor. If there was opportunity eventually to help out in the school when I felt strong enough, I could work there. They wanted to make sure that from the operation I had had in March, I had fully recovered.

I went up to Bukavu to have a rest and to teach in the school as it was considered a safe zone. In the meantime, after months of waiting without any knowledge of what had happened to me or even if I was still alive, my parents received a letter from AOG. It said in part:

Dear Mr. and Mrs. Lucas,

Our missionary secretary, Mr. Hawkins, arrived by air in Bujumbura at midday yesterday and has met all of our missionaries who have safely evacuated from the Congo Republic. This morning we received a cable from him which reads as follows:

"ARRIVED SAFELY. ALL WELL HERE. INFORM FAMILIES. PRAY. - HAWKINS"

What a relief that letter would have been for my parents!

20th December 1964

On Sunday 20th December we heard from the American missionaries that the American embassy had told the missionaries to be ready to evacuate at any time because the Mulaliste were regrouping and had sent replacements to the Congo via Rwanda and Burundi.

22nd December 1964

We missionaries (British, Swedish and American) who had been teaching in the school talked over the situation and planned who would be placed in the various cars so each would know which car to go to if it was a sudden evacuation.

24th December 1964

On Christmas Eve, at dinner time, a message was received from the USA consul that a military plane was arriving at 2pm and all women and children and anyone else who wanted must be ready to take it. We heard this at 1pm. I left the table, my dinner half eaten and got ready with several others, and we were driven out to the airfield. We were taken by plane to Leopoldville (now Kinshasa) and then on to the mission guesthouse. When I arrived there, I found that I had just missed seeing Olive McCarten, an old school friend from Dagenham who was also escaping from another part of the Congo.

Some of the missionaries held under house arrest (I was not in this photo as I was taking the photo with my camera!)

The American missionaries had arranged to take a plane going from Brazzaville to Amsterdam on the Friday flight. Planes were scheduled to run every Friday normally, but would they be flying at Christmas? Miraculously that was the case and there were places throughout the whole journey for the American missionaries. There was one spare place to Amsterdam, and I was asked if I would like to take it. "Yes please," I swiftly responded. There was a plane going to London that day, so I booked it. The man on the desk, said 'Ohhh... you're going to have a white Christmas!' I had a light summer dress on and had hardly anything with me as I had to escape so quickly. I burst out crying and the poor man who had no idea what the last six months had been like for me, shuffled me through to departures somewhat shocked.

I arrived at London airport and phoned Alfred Webb, the Pastor from Bethel Church in Dagenham. I asked him to warn my parents as they did not even know I was coming back. He spoke to me and said, 'Take the airport transport bus to the terminal' and he said he would pick me up. This was on Boxing Day! Mr. Webb met me and drove me home. Later that day, Mr. Webb visited Edith and Ken Thompson, close friends of mine in the Dagenham church and said, 'Guess who I saw today?' Immediately, Edith replied, 'Kathleen!' He asked how she knew, and she replied, 'Don't you remember? I was praying for Kathleen on Christmas Day!' It turned out that Edith had felt stirred to ask the church to pray for me on Christmas morning at the service and at that very moment I was saying yes to the spare seat on the plane!

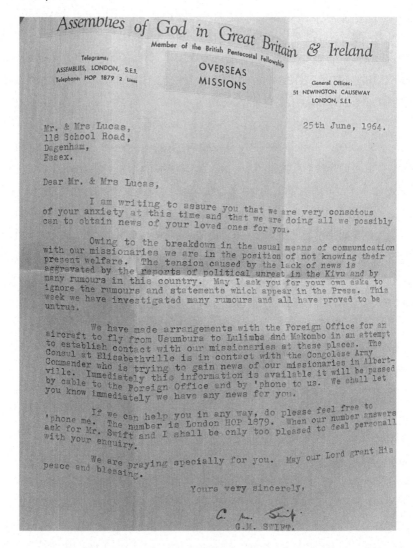

A letter sent to my parents in June 1964 to assure them that AOG were doing all they could to help us.

Assemblies of God in Great Britain & Ireland

Member of the British Pentecostal Fellowship

Telegrams:	OVERSEAS	General Offices:
ASSEMBLIES, LONDON, S.E.1.		51 NEWINGTON CAUSEWAY
Telephone: HOP 1879 2 Lines	MISSIONS	LONDON, S.E.1.

15th October, 1964.

Dear Mr. and Mrs. Lucas,

Our Missionary Secretary, Mr. Hawkins, arrived by air in Bujumbura at midday yesterday and has met all our missionaries who have safely evacuated from the Congo Republic.

This morning we received a cable from him which reads as follows:-

"ARRIVED SAFELY. ALL WELL HERE. INFORM FAMILIES. PRAY.

HAWKINS."

We know that you will be delighted to have this news and we are passing it on to you as quickly as possible. We assure you that as we are remembering our missionaries in prayer we are also remembering the members of their families for we appreciate the anxiety which you have felt during the past months.

In due course we expect to receive detailed information from our Missionary Secretary and will arrange for you to have this immediately. No doubt most of you will have received personal letters by now and if not you should do so in the next day or two.

Whilst Mr. Hawkins is in the Congo, I shall be looking after his office for him and if you wish to contact us on any matter do please feel free to do so.

Greetings and best wishes for the blessing of the Lord.

Yours very sincerely,

G.M. SWIFT.
General Treasurer.

A letter sent to my parents in October 1964 to assure them we had escaped safely.

Reflect...

Notice how often Kathleen shows gratitude for the small things in life. What are you grateful for today?

Kathleen held onto God's prophetic Word over her life which is what sustained her. What words have been said over your life or have you read in God's word that you can "hide in your heart?"

Chapter 8

Return to the Congo after the Troubles

1965 - 1966

'But those who hope in the Lord will renew their strength. They will soar on wings like eagles; they will run and not grow weary, they will walk and not be faint.' Isaiah 40:31

A service of thanksgiving, remembrance and prayer was planned to be held on Saturday 6th February 1965, in Westminster Chapel in London to honour those missionaries who tragically lost their lives in Congo between 1960-1964.

The Oversees Mission Council asked me to go and represent the Assemblies of God churches and to honour

Edmund ('Teddy') Hodgson & Elton Knauf of AOG churches who had been murdered. This was just one month after I had returned home and I remember taking the train up to London on my own, praying as I went that the Lord would help me. I just remember the power of God accompanying me as I travelled there. I spoke for just five minutes in honour of those who gave their lives.

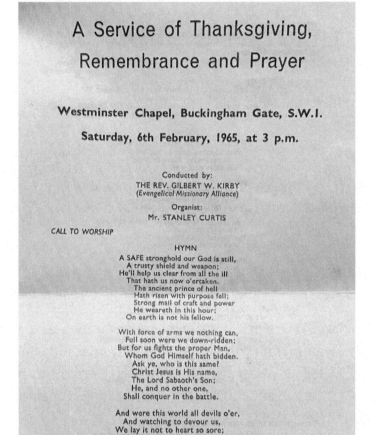

The service of Thanksgiving & Remembrance

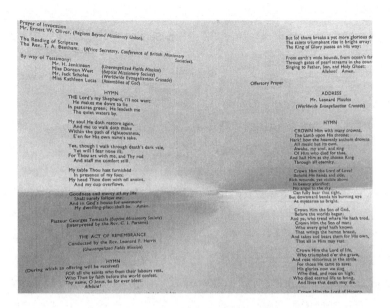

Prayer of Invocation
Mr. Ernest W. Oliver, (Regions Beyond Missionary Union).

The Reading of Scripture
The Rev. T. A. Beetham, (Africa Secretary, Conference of British Missionary Societies).

By way of Testimony:
Mr. H. Jenkinson   (Unevangelized Fields Mission)
Miss Doreen West   (Baptist Missionary Society)
Mr. Jack Scholes   (Worldwide Evangelization Crusade)
Miss Kathleen Lucas   (Assemblies of God)

HYMN
THE Lord's my Shepherd, I'll not want:
He makes me down to lie
In pastures green; He leadeth me
The quiet waters by.

My soul He doth restore again,
And me to walk doth make
Within the path of righteousness,
E'en for His own name's sake.

Yes, though I walk through death's dark vale,
Yet will I fear none ill;
For Thou art with me, and Thy rod
And staff me comfort still.

My table Thou hast furnishèd
In presence of my foes;
My head Thou dost with oil anoint,
And my cup overflows.

Goodness and mercy all my life
Shall surely follow me:
And in God's house for evermore
My dwelling-place shall be. Amen.

Pasteur Georges Tomatala (Baptist Missionary Society)
(Interpreted by the Rev. C. J. Parsons)

THE ACT OF REMEMBRANCE
Conducted by the Rev. Leonard F. Harris
(Unevangelized Fields Mission)

HYMN
(During which an offering will be received)
FOR all the saints who from their labours rest,
Who Thee by faith before the world confest,
Thy name, O Jesus, be for ever blest:
Alleluia!

But lo! there breaks a yet more glorious da
The saints triumphant rise in bright array:
The King of Glory passes on His way:

From earth's wide bounds, from ocean's far
Through gates of pearl streams in the coun
Singing to Father, Son, and Holy Ghost:
Alleluia! Amen.

Offertory Prayer

ADDRESS
Mr. Leonard Moulos
(Worldwide Evangelization Crusade)

HYMN
CROWN Him with many crowns,
The Lamb upon His throne;
Hark! how the heavenly anthem drowns
All music but its own.
Awake, my soul, and sing
Of Him who died for thee,
And hail Him as thy chosen King
Through all eternity.

Crown Him the Lord of Love!
Behold His hands and side,
Rich wounds, yet visible above
In beauty glorified;
No angel in the sky
Can fully bear that sight,
But downward bends his burning eye
At mysteries so bright.

Crown Him the Son of God,
Before the worlds began:
And ye, who tread where He hath trod,
Crown Him the Son of man!
Who every grief hath known
That wrings the human breast,
And takes and bears them for His own,
That all in Him may rest.

Crown Him the Lord of life,
Who triumphed o'er the grave,
And rose victorious in the strife
For those He came to save:
His glories now we sing
Who died, and rose on high;
Who died eternal life to bring,
And lives that death may die.

Crown Him the Lord of Heaven,

The programme for the service of Remembrance including
my name on behalf of Assemblies of God

From then on, I began to get letters from various London churches to give my testimony and eventually a full itinerary was arranged by the AOG. Although many were AOG churches, there were also many churches of other denominations in which I spoke. I remember when I was invited by the Church of England at St Albans. They gave me such a wonderful welcome. They were memorable occasions. They always stood out! I often travelled on my own to these churches sharing what God was doing in the Congo. However I soon found that the more I shared these experiences, and they were painful, the more I ended up telling the story as if I was removed from it. If I had allowed myself to feel the emotion, I would never have been able to share. Somehow, I separated myself from the story in order to be able to share it.

Return to Congo

Gradually, the situation in the Congo was becoming more settled and IPPKi, the teacher training school, had been reformed in Bukavu by September of 1965. David Pike and John Miles had already joined the staff in Bukavu. Beryl Gough had completed her obligatory colonial course in Belgium and was keen to join the IPPKi staff. We travelled out together early in January 1966. As usual we travelled via Brussels and stayed the weekend with Mr. and Mrs. Gunter. They themselves had a new flat and the elderly residents' home that I often visited had been enlarged and greatly improved. The day we arrived the council officials came with a belated New Year's present for the residents - toiletries and a huge box of biscuits for each person which brought them great joy. We had left our large luggage at the airport to be picked up on Monday. Fortunately, we had no difficulty when we arrived at the airport. Beryl sat with our hand luggage, and I went to redeem our large suitcases. We had no need to re-weigh luggage or hand luggage and no extra charges were made!

All the Protestant missionaries who were now, like us, operating in Bukavu rather than on isolated bush stations, gathered together for fellowship on a Saturday afternoon and these services were held at the Swedish mission in the 'Église Évangélique.' This was the church that had been developed over the years for French speaking Europeans and Asians. We now needed to look for accommodation and we were offered a two-bed bungalow situated by the lake which was partially furnished. For any other furniture we required we could place an order for it at a local technical school where the students were willing to make it for us.

We moved into the bungalow at the end of January and were pleasantly surprised that we not only had running water and electricity, but a telephone had been installed! We were living in luxury! Although the bungalow was a little way out of town, other missionaries were willing to take us to and from school each day. Later, a Swedish missionary sold us her car as she was going home on furlough which we were able to use.

General Mobutu, a general in the national army who would later become president, came to Bukavu at the end of February. As a result, there was a three-day holiday announced in his honour.

Visit from AOG to Assess the Mission after the Troubles
When we arrived in the Congo, we found Bukavu was calm and functioning reasonably well although houses were quite damaged from the troubles. We stayed at the Swedish mission for the first night and then on Sunday we went to the large church at Kadutu.

Walter Hawkins, the general secretary of the AOG Oversees Mission Council had been asked to evaluate our field. He arrived in Bukavu in late April 1966 and asked David Pike and myself to go with him to Albertville (Kalemie). We were chosen as we had been there for some time. We went to Albertville to try to contact our pastors there. The town was calm but full of mercenaries, Belgian advisors, and national army troops. At this time mercenaries were called by Belgian officials to help and were recognised as being on the side of the national troops. There were very few Europeans or traders in town. We were able to meet about 100 Christians in a village about 30 kilometres out of town. They told us that countless others remained in their hideouts in the bush or were still in rebel-controlled areas. Our mission was situated in a contested zone. We were, however, still able to have a service with these Christians and encourage them with the Word of God. We went along to the hospital to visit one of our pastors who had been shot five times and left for dead. He had several wounds and when we visited, he was still too weak to be operated on to have the last of the bullets removed from his thigh. At his bedside lay the four bullets that had been removed. They reported to us that Lulimba was now held by the national army, but rebels were still in the region. It was an interesting visit but very sad to hear such news. Of course, we were glad to get back to Bukavu. Early in May 1966, President Tshombe was out of government and so we wondered what this would lead to. (He had become president in 1964 after some time spent in exile in Northern Rhodesia and Spain, but was dismissed from his position in October 1965 around allegations of treason. The army chief Joseph Mobutu then seized power after staging a successful coup.)

Our post still took several weeks to arrive and was being censored (because of Tshombe being in power). In July the Kalembelembe pastors asked the mission to open a new school in Albertville to replace the one destroyed in Lulimba. As IPPKi was on holiday (it was July at this time) the four of us went to Albertville to discuss the possibilities for the future but it still felt too soon to make any definitive decisions. We tentatively explored the possibility of hiring a building to use as a classroom. We eventually went back to Bukavu.

In August 1966, Lemera was declared free of rebel activity. Medical help was desperately needed as you can imagine. The nurses returned to re-establish the dispensary and the maternity units, gradually extending the work and using the school dormitories as a hospital unit. It was eventually transformed into a hospital. Late September, the headteacher said we could all go along to Lemera for a surprise visit, so we excitedly travelled there. The mission houses seemed to be in a fair state although there was of course no furniture, and they were very dirty. The church roof had been damaged but still served its purpose. It was good to see my old home but living in the bush was well out of the question for now.

In November, the Swedes invited us to move house nearer to the mission as they had rented a house that was twice as large as the bungalow. It was within walking distance of both Norwegian and Swedish missions and nearer the school. This of course was a reasonable proposition, so we accepted their offer. Soon after the move, I had to make another trip to Albertville to regulate the legal situation. (When Tshombe came into power, he had declared that all the missions now had to be a united church). As I was the legal representative, I had to present all the necessary paperwork.

The situation in town was much better than in July but the interior was very troubled. Whilst I was there, I heard that two Roman Catholic priests were released by the national army troops after nearly three years of being held by the rebels. They were only 40km from Lulimba where we were under house arrest, but the national troops were given orders only to deal with our release and not theirs. This was all due to the strategic location because if they had been rescued and had gone up there, the rest of the people would have been trapped. They could not be released at the same time because the national army troops were given strict orders to deal with the Fizi road only and bring us out to safety - no digressions were allowed. The priests were in hospital for a checkup after their release but were otherwise well, which truly was remarkable!

Early in January 1967, the school library was replenished which was a great blessing. This was due to UNESCO and the Swedish and Norwegian governments who had all made contributions at the same time. John Miles (an AOG missionary from Bristol) began to make preparations for his wedding to Sarah, an American missionary working in

Bandaka. (They had met in Belgium whilst training). We were fascinated by all the formalities required for the wedding! He had to travel to Elisabethville (now Lubumbashi) because we had no consulate in Kivu province and so that was our nearest British consulate. They had to go there to sign so many forms and then, the Mayor of Gloucester was to read the banns in the public square on the morning of the wedding which seemed strange as we were so far away from there!

Second Visit from AOG to Assess the Mission Situation

Walter Hawkins planned another visit from February 11th - 28th to assess the situation here after all the troubles. John Miles and I were to accompany him. We took him to see Lemera on the Thursday and the following day after school, we took him to Bideka, a girls' school about 30 km outside town. From there, it was onto Burusa which had a woodwork school where they were training African carpenters.

On the Sunday after church, we took him up to the bamboo forest for a visit. Unfortunately, we did not see any elephants although we were told there were some in the area. On Monday we should have set off for Albertville but Mr. Hawkin's papers were not in order. The office promised to have everything ready by 9am on Monday morning and our plane was to leave at 11am over the border in Rwanda. We got there at 10.45am and Mr. Hawkins was given his papers, but it was too late for the plane. We hired a petite porteur (a small 5-seater plane) for Tuesday. Over the border the Catholic mission had a private plane that we often used. The flight took 30 minutes from Shangugu in Rwanda to Albertville. It was either that or a two day journey by boat.

American missionaries, Mary and Elma Deal had come back to Albertville. They were expecting us for days but failed to go out to the airport on the Tuesday because normally there was no flight on that day. When we arrived there was no one to meet us but fortunately military personnel who happened to be there offered to take us into town.

On Wednesday we made arrangements with the mercenaries to go to Lulimba. Major Shroeda said that we could have five armed mercenaries to go with us and they gave us a jeep and Landrover. We were meant to set off at midday on Thursday, but the mercenaries were on another assignment. They arrived at 4pm and had already been on the road for 48 hours. Now they were told to make themselves ready to make a return trip to Lulimba. The Landrover came to pick us for 4.30pm so we put our camping equipment on board and were taken to the arms depot to see the sergeant major and the other four who were to travel with us. The jeep was filled up with machine guns and off we went.

The lads were used to the road and so they just flew along missing all the potholes! It was a pleasure to travel on the roads and not feel the bumps! We got about 100 km outside town when we noticed that the wheel of the jeep was loose but not to worry - the sergeant major got out, went to the jeep and lifted the bodywork with one of the assistants. Whilst this was happening, another one tightened the screws with his fingers. I wrote to my mum regarding this 'if you want to see a strong man act, you do not have to go to the circus, trust me, join the mercenaries.'

We went as far as Bendera. The jeep was still playing up so they asked me to go to the garage there and ask if we could use it to fix the wheel properly. It was now 8.30pm. The jeep was on the bridge and the men set to work with a will to get it done. By 9.30pm they decided it would take too long to fix it properly. Two mercenaries with machine guns stayed behind to fix things properly and we set off for the rest of the journey.

The worst part of the road was before us, and we plunged into the mud quite often. Fortunately, we were in a four-wheel drive. It was 2.30am when we arrived. It was fortunate that we had the mercenaries with us as the national army troops were a little agitated to see a vehicle coming at this time of night. When they saw the mercenaries, they thought there would be trouble, but we spoke to them and calmed down the situation. I was always pushed ahead to speak in such situations. I think they hoped that the people may remember me and so this would help calm any uneasiness. I think they also believed it may have helped that I was a woman!

When we saw the houses, there were no doors or windows left. The roof was full of bullet holes. The small house had been demolished. Neither the maternity building nor the school dormitories had their roofs left in tact. Primary school children were sitting where the school used to be. It was so strange that they sat there as if wishing things were not as they were. All I can remember was disbelief and shock at what had happened. It was unbelievable to me that human beings could bring so much harm to one another.

We slept that night with the camping gear. The following day the pastors and teachers, as many as could come, were there but of course we could do very little with them as there were so few. They could only help distribute clothing and money. We had been trying to get salaries out to them. Everywhere we went, we had mercenaries guarding us. Many of them were very tall and constantly with rifles but they stayed with us the whole time. On Saturday we decided to leave around 10am. All was going well until we got about 20km outside Bendera. We hit a muddy stretch and the car suffered a puncture. We had no spare wheel this time. There was nothing else we could do but plod on with a flat tyre.

We went for five kilometres and came across an army truck on its way to Bendera. Once again, I had to go and ask if we could have a lift or to borrow a spare tyre. This time I was accompanied by three mercenaries. It was funny to see how seriously they took the job of looking after me. I suppose they fully understood the dangers to me, to John Miles and

Walter Hawkins, and the other mercenaries. We left the other men on the road to come with the crippled car and the army lorry. At Bendera there was no spare wheel, so we begged and pleaded for a new inner tube and outer cover. They spent two hours fixing the inner tube, patching it, and reshaping the wheel as it had been driven with a flat tyre. We set off at 5pm and arrived at 9.30pm covered in dust and mud but glad to get back to civilisation.

Whilst at Lulimba it was so sad to see the damaged buildings, but even worse was to see the lack of young people aged between 20 and 30. So many of them must had been killed during the rebellion.

We eventually came back to Bukavu. Air Congo prices were extremely cheap which made it possible for Beryl and myself to travel with John Miles and his best man, Ingamar Blom to attend the wedding in Bandaka.

It took us a week on different planes to get to the area where the wedding would be held. The wedding took place and then we returned quickly. This time Sarah came with us because she had to get back to her teaching. They were married but separated after the honeymoon at Bukavu.

Independence Celebrations Cause a Stir
In April, the teachers heard that there might be a free government ticket home for the holidays so Beryl was expecting to have one. I was not included as I was not in full time teaching at the time but running back and forth to

Albertville trying to sort out legalities as the legal representative. Beryl would go home on 18 July and I was asked to spend that summer for about three or four months in Albertville to plan for the school.

We had just the one car now at the mission between us all and John, who lived in another part of town, often had the car. He came on the evening of the 21st June to visit. As he turned into our road, a jeep travelling in the other direction without lights plunged straight into him. Fortunately, nobody was hurt but naturally a jeep with an iron bar in front of it meant our car was badly damaged.

At the Italian garage the mechanic said it would take 2 weeks to repair. Who knew how long that really meant! That was June 21st. If our car was in the garage for two weeks that would take us to 30th June 1967, which was the day of the independence celebrations.

On 1st July, we all went to town to witness the Independence Day parade. Firstly, the military in new uniforms, then in various groups, school children with flags, nurses with placards and slogans, football teams and dancers in national dress. It certainly was a spectacular occasion.

A day or two later, gunshots were heard, and we wondered what was happening. A rumour went out that it was just a military practice. At the Swedish mission there was a row of buildings with missionary accommodation and then a formation of offices and printing press. There was also a mission radio where we sent radio broadcasts in various languages preaching the gospel. Another area was turned into accommodation which we nicknamed 'the convent' for 6 single women. What Majken Bergman records happening on that day is as follows:-

"At 7am one morning at the beginning of July, we heard strong gunfire. What can that be? A rumour was that it was only an army practice. It was calm for several hours and then we heard that a group of mercenaries had caused an uproar in the national army camp. They left the army camp and journeyed out into the bush. The national army troops began to look for the enemy. Why had this happened? All of these mercenaries were white and armed men who were armed with weapons and so the national army thought all white men would be against them. Added to that naturally, radio Bukavu began to send out messages that it was best for everybody to arm themselves. Having heard that on the news, in 'the convent' and mission they thought it was best that they remain indoors. Soldiers began to look throughout the town, going from house to house hunting mercenaries who may be hiding. One afternoon, the mission received visitors from the army to control and to see what was happening. When they saw white people gathered, they began to get excited with their weapons and they called out 'open the door!' The missionaries shouted 'we are missionaries'. Of course, missionary and mercenary sound similar and they began to get more and more excited. Normally that would have calmed things down by saying

'missionary' but of course they had misunderstood. Someone shouted out 'we are not soldiers, we are people carrying God's message.' It finally registered and was calm for the rest of the afternoon. When they left, the missionaries realised it was a dangerous situation as the soldiers would go away, drink alcohol and most certainly come back. The missionaries had a moment of prayer and decided it was time they began to prepare to leave but they ended up staying another two weeks under house arrest. They finally left for Shangugu."

Another Escape out of the Country

As soon as there was less military activity in town, the pastors and elders pleaded with the missionaries to return to Europe (alive!) and come back when the conditions improved. Beryl and I had no idea what had taken place at the mission. We had also heard the military gunfire and concluded it was a normal military practice. We decided to keep a low profile and remain indoors.

Later that day American missionaries Nadine Schik and Helen Gow called to say that a military plane was on its way to Shangugu (now Cyangugu) and all Americans were ordered to leave for the airport.

Knowing that our car was in the garage they promised to take us over the border with them. Others promised to take care of John. As we approached the border, we came under gunfire but praise God, there were no casualties.

When we arrived at the airfield, the American consul was already preparing to explain the evacuation procedure. He firmly announced that all single women would be transported to Nairobi and be catered for by the American UN personnel there. Only men and married couples would continue to Kinshasa.

This presented a problem for a young American couple. They were due to marry a little later in the year and naturally did not want to be separated! The consul came up with a solution. Radio contact was made with the military plane en-route and the flight captain confirmed that he was qualified to conduct a wedding! The missionaries hastily prepared the ceremony. As soon as the plane touched down in Shangugu we celebrated the very unusual airfield wedding. John Miles bade farewell to us and travelled to Kinshasa to join his wife Sarah who was at her mission in that area. Nadine, Helen, Beryl and myself were well looked after in Nairobi for a couple of days.

The next thing I remember is returning home to England in August 1967 where I began itinerating once again.

Reflect...

When Kathleen returned to the Congo, she was able to visit various places seeing the devastation that took place. In the world we now live, we see devastation so often on our TV's or social media that there can be a risk of us becoming desensitised. How can you ensure you do not become desensitised to the pain around you?

Chapter 9

Final Years in the Congo

1967 - 1970

'Remember not the former things, neither the things of old. Behold, I will do a new thing. Now it shall spring forth!' Isaiah 43:18-19

Filadelfia Church in Stockholm, invited Per-olof Jacobsson to give a report following his discussion with pastors and government officials in Bukavu that was held in December 1967. The report was accepted as favourable, and missionaries began to return. Beryl Gough and I returned on August 28th 1968.

We travelled from London to Brussels and on to Kigali and then in the small 5-seater plane from Kigali to Shangugu (now Cyangugu). Daniel Halldorf (the Director of the school) and Alfred Tobler (a missionary in Shangugu) met us at the airport. Alfred invited us to coffee while we waited for our luggage to arrive on a following plane. The luggage came at 4.30pm. By the time we reached the border it was almost time for the immigration office to close. Daniel suggested we give the officials a lift into town. There was wisdom in this generous offer as our passports were swiftly stamped and nobody had time to inspect the luggage for hidden weapons as the office was being locked for the night!

A large group of well-wishers met us at the airport to commit us to the Lord. We were invited to stay at the mission until December and then we would need to look for alternative accommodation as a family was expected in the New Year who would need our rooms. Security had been enhanced at the mission. Iron bars were now fitted to all windows and doors and huge metal gates at the entrance to the compound. A few weeks later, we had evidence that these precautions were needed. We were disturbed one night by a loud splintering of glass. Someone had broken the windows and helped themselves to the curtains, so we sellotaped paper to the windows to hinder further loss.

A New Home
We located an empty house near the mission that was being repaired. The owner promised to complete the work by mid-December and also put bars at the doors and windows. In September, a young Norwegian missionary was suddenly taken ill and was vomiting and haemorrhaging. The Norwegian doctor diagnosed a stomach ulcer and asked us all to be ready to donate blood. Four of us were

group 0. A provisional blood donor unit was set up in the Norwegian mission where we each donated blood direct to the patient twice a day for three consecutive days. Still the doctor feared for his life. A group of pastors came to pray and fast. Praise God! Within days he was able to sit up and four or five weeks later he was back in school teaching!

In October, Hilda Backlund, a Swedish missionary was honoured by the state for long service. She was decorated with a medal for her 40 years of service to the country. When she came from Goma with her medal, we all celebrated with her. How amazing that despite all the military activities and upheavals such a ceremony should take place and that they could trace the records that far back!

A Miracle of Resources

When Beryl and I came back in August, we were handed a pile of dirty, muddy papers that had been brought to the mission from our house when we fled. At first, I thought they were only fit to be thrown away, but on closer inspection these papers revealed hidden treasures. First, Beryl found a set of stencilled history notes that would help her for the sixth form examinations. Secondly, Sven Erik Grön, the legal representative for the Swedish mission, lacked staff for the Bible School and decided that he would have to send the newly arrived students back to the villages until Christmas. On the Monday morning, he went along to the school, spent time with the students, had a time of prayer and came back to the mission with tears in his eyes. He said, 'I didn't have the courage to tell them to go home!' It was then that I found, among the hidden treasures, some Bible correspondent courses that Barbara and Cyril Cross had sent across from the Nairobi Bible College before our evacuation in 1967. These could be used to occupy the students until new staff arrived. At the same time, a young children's evangelist working in Burundi, promised to come and hold a few lectures.

Way back in 1965, an order was given that all missions had to renew their legal standing 'Personalité Civil'. We, together with others, submitted our documents. Our papers were returned as being incomplete time and time again. The documents were returned as incomplete or delayed in the post or not even recognised as being part of a mission as we were in a contested zone, still rebel held. Now at the end of August we received a letter to say that if our documents were not regulated before 31st December 1968, the mission would be dissolved. Once again, I discovered something amongst all the dirty documents, I found a letter with a list of names for all our pastors with all their signatures. This was the very document we needed that would certainly help. I began to clean the paper with a rubber and then made a photostat copy. Praise God! None of the dirty marks were reproduced. Armed with this letter, Beryl and I set off to Kinshasa to resubmit our claims. Fortunately, missionaries were given free flights on military planes to the capital, so it was a far easier journey. We visited several general offices, but nobody was available to see us. Finally, on the 20th December at the Congo Council, the secretary obtained an interview for us with the Minister of Justice. There we heard that our papers had reached his office. Our mission was in order and his letter of approval would be prepared for the following week. It was running dangerously close to the end of the year. As we were to wait another week in Kinshasa, we decided to regulate medical and school documents whilst there. Things were not straightforward, and more documentation was required from the local authorities! I would need to return in the New Year!

A Visit with Missionaries in Kinshasa

The Sunday before Christmas, Jaques Vernaud and his wife, ex-students of IBTI had invited us to their church service. They had been there for three years in Kinshasa. We were also invited to celebrate Christmas and the New Year with them. They told us at Christmas that they had baptised over 3000 people since being there. It was wonderful spending time with them. On 4th January the Minister of Justice signed our letter of approbation and we flew back to Bukavu. There were no seats on the plane as it was a military one, but only metal strips attached to the wall. At Kisangani, the national army troops filled the plane. The pilots, one American and the other a South African, invited Beryl and I into the cockpit. As a result, we had comfortable seats all the way to Goma. We stayed the night at the mission in Goma and then went back to Bukavu the following day.

We had been in Kinshasa three weeks and were looking forward to moving into our new home. Imagine our dismay when we discovered that bandits had entered the house. When the night watchman arrived, he was drunk. In the midst of all this discouragement, the Lord gave me a promise. I read Isaiah 43:18-19, *"Remember not the former things, neither the things of old. Behold, I will do a new thing. Now it shall spring forth!"* The Lord was telling me to forget and not dwell on the past events. Events like independence 1960, devastation of the rebellion 1964 or the mercenary attack in 1967. He was about to do a new thing for the mission! I felt encouraged. We had wonderful help to clean up the mess, new locks fitted, and iron bars were now fitted on the balcony which was the weak point where the bandits had climbed up over the wall into the balcony and opened the doors. We were glad that we'd not moved all our belongings to the house before going to Kinshasa - we would have had nothing left.

Infestation of the 'Jiggers!'
In the house we had become infested with 'Jiggers' (Chiggers). These are small tropical sand fleas that burrow beneath the skin laying their egg sacks and causing sores. I normally managed to remove them but one day I had one right under my foot that I couldn't reach so I asked the boy that came to help us around the house to take it out for me and offered him a needle. Normally I would light a match, hold it to the needle to clean it and it would not poison me. When I gave him the needle, he looked at me as if I was mad. "You don't remove jiggers with a needle," was his remark! "You only break the sack and get more jiggers." Off he went to the kitchen and came back with a carving

knife. I thought he intended an amputation. Beryl came out of her bedroom just in time to see 'Dr Laurent' remove the jigger and egg sack neatly from my foot and I did not feel a thing. We paid Laurent to provide security and help with some of the work we needed done, but, I did not expect, and I'm sure he did not either, that he would have to help get jiggers out of my feet. From this point on we ensured we had creosote in the water when we washed the floors and even the garage floors to keep the jiggers away! That went down every day to kill them so that I did not have to have a repeat performance of the kitchen knife.

Backwards and Forwards to Kinshasa

As soon as we returned from Kinshasa, I contacted the local education office regarding state recognition for our schools. There were 3 schools in every area where we had an evangelist.

After an exchange of letters and many visits to various offices, we were finally granted a letter of approbation by the provincial officer of the district in what was then still a contested zone. This letter came a week before Easter. Beryl and I set off for Kinshasa again. It was kind of her to come along with me during her holidays.

We thought that everything would be settled within the two weeks, but oh no! Beryl had to return to Bukavu in time for the new school term and I remained to continue the business. Daily, I went along to the administration buildings to plead my case. On April 26th, I was granted an audience with the Minister of Education who very graciously signed the 'Convention Scolaire'. This really was an answer to prayer as our mission was in a contested zone and as a result was politically unwelcome.

During this season, I occasionally taught and at other times I helped out at the Bible School, but a great deal of my time was taken up with getting everything in order to be able to deal with the legal side of things. I knew that someone had to do this even though it was frustrating at times. I also had the benefit of meeting other missionaries working throughout the country.

The Bible School held their graduation service at the end of May. Phares Kachunga, one of our mission students was chosen to represent the student body. He gave a great word in the church service. We were so glad that he was to begin his work as an evangelist at Mtoa along the lakeside. Rosalie Hegi was delighted to learn about this because it was happening in a place she had worked for many years. She would have been delighted to receive the first Bible School student.

We tried to capture the broadcast of the moon landing in July 1969, but reception was very indistinct. I felt so sorry for our American friends at the mission who were so eager to see it. They consoled themselves saying that their families would send a detailed account.

Visitors from the UK

The Norwegian government had offered to pay for the new school that was being built in Bukavu for IPPKi. It was planned to be ready for September 1970. My Pastor from Dagenham, Alfred Webb, Lesley Botham and Idris Parry from the AOG mission's department came out to visit in August. They arrived at different times. We wanted to be able to show them the different work that was taking place across the region. So, we begun with the new school

A visit from pastors from the UK

building and other missions' stations to give them an idea of the full extent of work done in the area including setting up medical facilities and schools. As part of the trip, we took the three visitors on an old steamboat to visit some of the areas.

The boat was in a state of disrepair but full of people. The toilets were overflowing. It was quite a shock for Alfred, a travelling glove salesman with a particular love for his clothes. This was his first time.

I wrote this letter to all my mission supporting churches about the time that we had visitors from the UK including my Pastor. We wanted to explain to them all the work that was taking place.

"First of all, we went to the new school in Bukavu. Miss Gough and I have been teaching in IPPKi for several years now, but during the recent civil war the school was totally destroyed, and we were forced to teach from borrowed buildings. Last year the Norwegian government wanted to

help the Congolese people and so granted us money for new buildings. This new school is far better than anything that we could have erected as a group of missionaries. It is situated on the top of one of the mountains overlooking Lake Kivu. I am sure many children in England would love to attend such a school. We went on to visit Bideka, where we have a school for young ladies. From Bideka we went along to Burhusa, another Norwegian mission station where boys are trained in carpentry and other crafts. We are glad to have this professional school so near to Bukavu. Our tables and chairs were made there. After the civil war our houses were looted and we lost everything, but thanks to Burhusa school we were soon able to re-furnish our home. Whilst at Burhusa we had the joy of hearing the missionary explain to our visitors that he was faced with a problem - the church was too small. They have over 1500 members and their new church, which had opened in 1966, already needs to be extended. It looks as if the Christians on that station have been busy telling others of the Saviour.

A day or two later we took our visitors on to Kaziba to the Norwegian hospital. We were moved as we went from one hospital ward to another. So many sick and suffering. Although the rebellion dissipated, its effects were still evident. We were particularly saddened by a group of very young children suffering from kwashiorkor, a disease caused by malnutrition.

Many of these children had to hide in the bush for long periods and thus lacked the normal diet. Their limbs were *very thin and tiny, their hair bore different shades of red or grey. Some, because of advanced disease, were bald. Many of these children were too ill to walk. One young girl in particular caught my attention, she was about twelve years of age. When we looked at her face she looked just like an old, old granny, she had a head scarf on to keep her warm, her sunken cheeks broke into a pathetic smile as she said 'Jambo' or 'good morning'. Her arms and legs were the thinnest I have ever seen. Doctor Orlein, with tears in his eyes, said that the child would never walk. He says she may gain a little weight, but humanly speaking her condition will not improve greatly. This child is looking to the Lord for healing. Will you add your prayers to hers?*

A young United Nation's engineer has recently returned from a tour of inspection along the new road, and he has reported such pathetic conditions. For instance, in some villages only women and children remain, and they are living skeletons. Many of these women are our Christians - I wonder what type of houses they are living in if there are no men to rebuild the homes destroyed during the rebellion. All along this road there are military camps. The soldiers are there for the safety of the people, but this presents us with a new challenge. Many of these soldiers come from unevangelised regions and we need to meet them with the gospel. Pray with us that our local pastors and evangelists will be able to travel unhindered along the new road and that they will be able to hold services in the military camps....."

The letter then continued to outline some of the situations we were facing as missionaries and how we had shown the visitors around to give them context of the need.

On one occasion we went up to the baboon forest. We could hear gorillas but not see them! This was a research centre where they were officially looking after gorillas, chimpanzees, and baboons. As far as I was aware they were supplying Cape Kennedy with space craft experiments. This research centre, called the 'Karisoke Research Centre' was founded in 1967 to study endangered gorillas.

A Trip to Nairobi, Kenya
I travelled to Nairobi as I'd been having problems with my teeth for a long time. The dentist in Bujumbura suggested that to ease the sensitivity, I use emoform which was a type of toothpaste that could help. By October, the pain was still troubling me, and so I decided to visit Nairobi where Barbra Cross booked an appointment with a Christian dentist working for the Seventh Day Adventists.The dentist examined my teeth, polished, and cleaned them. He said there were no cavities and that my teeth were in perfect condition. He couldn't understand the sensitivity but said it was possibly due to lack of vitamins and the discolouration was due to the emoform. Another miracle - there was nothing seriously wrong!

Before I left for Nairobi, we heard that we needed to apply for new passports so this would be a good opportunity for me to do this. Prior to leaving I had visited some of my schoolboys in their dormitory. I realised how long their walk to school was and in the rainy season they regularly got very wet. Whilst in Nairobi one day we noticed plastic raincoats for sale in a Duka (a local market stall) so we bought them each one. They really were too long but that was an advantage - more protection for their trousers! There were caps to go with them and these caused more excitement than the raincoats. We laughed as they set off for school but at least they were dry!

Home in Bukavu

Our house in Bukavu, had a large basement which was probably meant to be used as a games room, but we turned it into a dormitory for the boys. In December 1969, Mobutu Sees Seko, the President of Congo came to Bukavu, and the town had been prepared for his visit. New streetlights had even been installed. The local population were anxious about this visit as they feared that attempts might be made on his life. On December 24th, Mobutu came to the football stadium where he was to address the public. Sadly, there was a rush to enter when the gates were opened, and all crowd control was lost. Thirty one died in the stampede. Many others were injured. Rumours had been spreading that the president's visit would cause trouble, but nobody expected such a tragedy.

In February 1970, Beryl and I went along to Kalemie (formally Albertville) to encourage our workers there. We were pleased that boat trips were out of the question. The new Bukavu airport was functioning and there were flights from Bukavu to Kalemie. I went along to the local Kalemie Department of Education to make more requests for the school papers because in the July visit our schools would be commencing in Kalemie. There was also to be a Bible school there, but formalities needed to be regulated in Kinshasa. It was to be another Kinshasa trip for me. What I thought would be dealt with in a short time in the capital became a series of five weeks of interviews in the ministerial offices. I returned to Bukavu in April, still not knowing the outcome of the negotiations.

King Baudouin and Queen Fabiola from Belgium came to visit Congo as it was ten years since it had gained its independence from their rule. Bukavu was to be included in the royal visit. It was a joy to see the welcome that they received.

My Time in the Congo Comes to a Sudden End
1970 was a year of great changes for Protestant missions in Congo. In February, Mobuto announced a 'One Church' state. It was to be called 'Eglise du Christ au Zaire' (Church of Christ in Zaire). This caused much discussion amongst the Protestant missions as we were concerned about the church and schools becoming part of a 'One Church' state. This would be similar to what had happened previously in China which caused a great deal of problems and persecution for the church and so we expected it to affect the Congo in the same way. Mobutu had been hugely influenced by Chinese ideas and so I am sure this played some part in this change.

At the same time, Bible schools were being told that they had to become Institutes of Theology under the state. The Oversees Mission's Council of AOG was aware of the situation and had asked Idris Parry and Walter Hawkins to join me in July and call our African workers to a conference in Kalemie. After long talks with our pastors, it was agreed that the kindest decision was to hand our work over to our African leaders. Walter Hawkins and I travelled down to Kalemie to see the pastors to discuss the situation of 'One Church'.

All Bible schools under this law would need to have teachers with theological degrees but we had people in the Bible college who had not even been to secondary school due to a lack of education in the country. There were strong discussions over the location of the Bible School. Many people wanted a Bible School in the Baraka area and not amongst the Wabembe. Frictions were still high between people with many still against the Wabembe due to what had happened during the rebellion. There was friction even amongst the Christians because of what people there had been through.

Beryl had already felt that God was calling her to study medicine and so she had booked her place on a plane to travel home on 13th July 1970. At the time that this was all happening, I was planning to go down to Kalemie and start the main secondary school there. Everything was packed and ready to go! Earlier in the year Beryl and I had been ordering and buying school materials for the school that was due to open. These were all packed in large wooden crates, ready to be shipped down to Kalemie. I was able to transfer the crates to the custom's shed in Bukavu, have them transported to Uvira and then by lake steamer to Kalemie. At the back of my mind was the promise of people who were meant to be coming from the UK to help at this school. Due to all the changes happening, my time in Congo came to a very abrupt end and I had to return to England.

As soon as Idris Parry and Walter Hawkins returned home from their time with us, I began the transition process. This meant several visits to Kinshasa between July and November to regulate the 'Personalité Civil' (legal status) and to try to regulate school matters. The legal documents were finally signed in October, and I was able to travel home on 29th November 1970.

Before returning to England, Walter Hawkins suggested that I join the staff at the Nairobi Bible school and teach English. My training was not in teaching English, and I really did not feel this was God's will for me, so I declined the request. At the same time, I was asked by Simon Petterson, to move to Gisenyi in Rwanda and help them there. He had started a Bible School there and was also running a secondary school. Knowing them and the foundation on which they had built there, I accepted. I flew home to the UK on 29th November 1970 and so my time in the Congo came to an end. I had spent 12 years in the beautiful but troubled country of Congo. Although things had ended quite unexpectedly, I had a real sense of God's will in my relocation to Rwanda. As Beryl and I became aware about the pending changes, we planned a day of prayer together which helped me spiritually prepare for the changes that were about to come.

My first class at the teacher training college in the Congo which had the first ever women to trained

A visit to see some younger children in the villages that had church connected to the Lemera Church.

Reflect...

Some seasons of life come to a sudden end. How do you deal with change?

How can you ensure you prepare well for transition moments in life?

Chapter 10

Onto Rwanda

1970 - 1972

"Then the word of the Lord came to Elijah: "Leave here, turn eastward and hide in the Kerith Ravine, east of the Jordan. You will drink from the brook, and I have directed the ravens to supply you with food there." 1 Kings 17:2

I had a complete rest at home with my parents for the month of December after returning from Zaire (formally The Congo). The oversees mission offices for AOG had now re-located to Nottingham and in due course I was invited to meet with the Oversees Mission Council where again it was suggested that I join the staff at Nairobi Bible School. I explained that I did not feel this was God's will for me and mentioned that Simon & Zelma Petterson were now working in Rwanda and had invited me to join them and help Dorcas Asplund with a new school project there. This is where I felt the Lord would have me work. This was a little problematic as it was not an AOG project but a Swedish mission project.

One day, I received a telegram from Stockholm from the Filadelfia church asking me to phone them. We had no telephone at home but as Alfred Webb, the pastor of Bethel Church in Dagenham was in America and William Hartley, an itinerant evangelist, was replacing him during his absence, I asked if I could use the phone in the church manse.

Filadelfia church had asked me to teach in a college in Burundi where I would be fully supported by the Swedish mission. I didn't feel that this was God's will either, but they asked me to think about it and phone again the following week. Although William Hartley was not present during the phone call, he could see that I was confused. I explained the situation and I remember him saying to me, 'Kathleen, when my wife and I get a letter asking us to take meetings for them and give us a date, if that date is clear in our diary, we write a little note to occupy the date. Should a subsequent offer come later for the same date, we know in our minds from our diary that that date is occupied and so we can't accept.' He then quoted Psalm 15:4 which says, *'The one who God honours keeps his oath even when it hurts.'* I felt this was the word that I needed. I now had an answer for both Stockholm and for the Oversees Mission's Council. Knowing that Gisenyi was the will of God for me, I planned to travel out in July 1971. The scripture that I felt God gave me in my final days in England was from 1Kings 17:2-4, *'Then the word of the Lord came to Elijah: "Leave here, turn eastward, and hide in the Kerith Ravine, east of the Jordan. You will drink from the brook, and I have directed the ravens to supply you with food there".'* A promise of God's provision to come.

The Journey onto Rwanda

As in 1968, I phoned the Protestant Council in Brussels and asked for them to arrange my ticket from Kigali onto Gisenyi. They said my ticket would be left at the airport in Brussels. When I arrived in Brussels, I made enquiries about my ticket and was told that it had not been left at the airport but would be delivered at 9.30pm in the evening. I changed some money, and as I was having something to eat and drink later in the day a Belgian lady asked if I was going on the evening flight to Kigali. I said yes and her next question rather shook me for she asked if I thought I would get through with all my luggage as they were restricted to 20kgs on the evening flight and there were no other flights that day! I phoned the mission office in Brussels, and they said they knew nothing about the restriction. Once again, there was a challenge with the weight of the baggage. I thought I would be alright with the 30kgs as I would ensure I had 10kgs in my hand luggage and 20kgs in my main bag. When it came to the check in, I had more than 20kgs and the airport official would not accept my luggage. In perfect timing, along came a representative from another mission's organisation. He said 'let her pass' and I managed to get on my way with all my baggage.

I arrived in Kigali and knew I had to pay for a small plane to Gisenyi which I had been warned about in Brussels. The pilot of the small plane asked for my payment. I said I was willing to pay for this short hop which was only a 10-minute flight. I certainly wanted to pay and get to Gisenyi that same day rather than hang about. A Roman Catholic priest heard me and asked if I was going to be on the 'special flight' out from Brussels and onto Gisenyi. I said 'yes' and he turned to the pilot and said to him 'include her on the list and bill the mission'. I now realised that I was on a special Roman Catholic chartered flight. The plane was full of priests and parents, and family members of priests who were working in Zaire or Rwanda. This was to be just the beginning of God's incredible provision.

Several months later, I received a letter from the AOG treasurer saying 'we've not yet received the bill for your ticket from the Protestant Council in Brussels. We have transferred the sum of money to your account.' A few more weeks went by and completely by chance I met the Swedish Baptist missionary who had been working in Brussels in the Protestant Council office. I remarked that I had not received my bill. He replied 'Oh! Your request came at the same time 'Raptim', (the Catholic mission's organisation that paid for my flight) had offered us free flights to Rwanda. They had so many tickets and it just so happened that it came at the same time as you were needing a ticket'. Elijah was cared for by ravens and then by the widow at Zarephath. (1 Kings

17:8&9) - both were unlikely sources, but I noted that this was the Lord's direction, *'I have directed the ravens...'*

A Short Trip back to Congo

I had finally arrived in Gisenyi, and I was to live with Dorcas Asplund, a Swedish missionary. She had been working in Burundi but had moved to Gisenyi to learn the local language. Some of my belongings had been left in drums in Bukavu. If I did not go back, I imagined these would be given away. So, in September I took the opportunity to go back to retrieve some of my belongings. At the same time, I would be able to see the progress that had been made on the school being built by the Norwegian government. It was situated in a beautiful part of town. Already several houses were completed for married couples and several apartments for single women members of staff. Even dormitories for the students had been completed. The town itself had undergone some changes too. A fleet of single buses were now operating in the area and pedestrian crossings were painted on several roads with police standing by with whistles in hand ready to signal anyone failing to cross in the right place (and to impose a fine, if they didn't).

Settling into Gisenyi

Dorcas and I began to settle into the home we were sharing together. From my bedroom window I could see the volcano in Zaire (now DRC) which was in the Virunga Mountains. One evening the sky was vivid red over the crater and on that occasion, we could actually see flames but even when there were no flames, we could always see a steady stream of smoke outlined on the horizon. The Virunga Mountains are a volcanic range north of Lake Kivu extending about 50 miles along the borders of the Democratic Republic of Congo, Rwanda, and Uganda. It contains eight major volcanic peaks.

We had no fridge, but a delivery driver came one evening from a station near the Ugandan border. He had brought material to Gisenyi and a fridge had been left behind by a missionary going home on furlough. He said we could use it although it was very old (more provision!).

As well as teaching here in Gisenyi I sometimes went over to Goma in Zaire (formally the Congo) to teach in the mission school there. Whilst I was there, I could buy meat and fish now that we had a fridge. In Gisenyi, we had plenty of fresh fruit and vegetables including buckets of small wild strawberries which were so tasty. An assortment of eggs were transported in banana skins. We were obviously always hoping for fresh eggs. We had to have water to see if the eggs would float or sink to determine if we could use them.

The people in Gisenyi were extremely poor. Each Friday was dedicated to food distribution for the elderly and disabled people who were unable to work in their gardens. Usually, they received a dish of dried beans to take home to cook and five francs to buy a little food of their choice.

On 16th November 1970, a consignment of clothing arrived from Sweden. We distributed them to local people. The people even put on hospital gowns and danced for joy! Disused operating garments and hospital blankets had been donated by hospitals in Sweden. Those hospitals were very particular so if they had a stain that could not be completely removed, they would send it on to go to missions' organisations for the poor. What was not good enough for one person was a real blessing for those we were ministering to in Rwanda.

Christmas in Burundi

A census of Europeans was declared and all passports were to be in Kigali between the 20th and 23rd December 1970. As Dorcas and I were going to Burundi for Christmas to celebrate with Ebba Hagstrand (she was helping with refugees previously in Lemera, Congo), her sister and nieces, all from the same church in Sweden, we decided to take all the passports of the Gisenyi missionaries up to Kigali with us. We needed a visa for Burundi in our own passports. We also needed ours to travel but having all the others with us was a problem as we needed to get them back to Gisenyi to their owners. We found a solution. We took all the Gisenyi passports with us to the Swiss mission family who were going to Gisenyi for Christmas so they could return them to their owners. To leave people without their passports was a challenge in case there was a situation in which they needed to escape quickly, and we obviously understood having lived through the rebellion in the Congo how easily this could happen.

Christmas Eve 1971 was a delightful reunion with Ebba and her sister. On Christmas Day, following the early morning church service, we went along to Lake Tanganyika to attend a baptismal service where about 50 people were baptised. Two hippos were quite visible in the bay! They were enjoying a peaceful laze in the sunshine, and we certainly did not want to disturb them.

On 27th December we began our journey back to Gisenyi via Bukavu. We spent the day with Madeleine Zbinden who was now well settled in her new bungalow at Bwindi at the new IPPKi school site that the Norwegians had built.

A Gift of Seeds from the UN

Early in the year, we received a quantity of vegetable seeds from South Africa via the United Nations. They thought we could try growing them because of the climate in the area we were living in. We planted lettuce, carrots, leaks, cucumber, and celery. According to our African friends, we had planted our garden too late in the season but by mid-January we began to reap fine results and had a daily supply of fresh vegetables for several weeks.

My 38th birthday was celebrated in style by friends on the mission station and during the afternoon coffee session Zelma Petterzon recited a poem that she had written in Swedish. As we all knew, Zelma had many talents. Composing poems was one of them. And here is a portion of it, of course translated into English from Swedish.

"Now I will honour you and celebrate your day. We are all glad to have you in our midst. I have many happy memories of earlier times when we could laugh often, and all was light and free. Up in Lemera's hilltop each day was bright and calm. But storm clouds came and there was trouble and strife. We had to leave that place. We went our separate ways. We are now doubly glad to have found you again. Here to our Rwanda you've been led. And God will bless you in this little land. Among the young people, you have a great task ahead. Your influence is greater than you think. You are so calm by nature, and you have a warm heart You don't hold grudges and unkindness. We take your hand and thank God for you."

I was always blessed by Zelma's poems. They would often be put to the tune of a well-known hymn. Although you cannot read the flow of words as it was spoken due to the translation you will be able to hear and feel the heart behind it and how it blessed me so much!

Practicalities of Living
New electric cables had been laid in town and we no longer had flickering lamps in the evening, but we still kept our paraffin lamps to hand in case of a power failure which happened often.

The price of food was increasing rapidly. Dorcas and I decided to go along to Kisoro over the border in Uganda. What a day we had! It was a joy to go into the one and only

Asian shop and stock up on food supplies at only a quarter of the price we had to pay in Gisenyi. When we arrived home late in the evening, I felt like I had been in all the shops in Oxford Street in London. It had been such a successful day. That was the only trip we made there.

Church Growth

It was always great to hear of new churches being opened in Rwanda. In February, a new church was opened in Buyoga which was situated way up in the mountains off the main Ruhengeri Kigali Road. What a road it was! Dorcas and I planned to spend a few days with the missionaries before the actual inauguration of the church. It was a good idea to have gone there in advance as the journey that normally took five hours took us eight hours due to heavy rains. At one point we had to sit and wait until the fog cleared before proceeding with our journey. Our friends were greatly encouraged by our visit and so we were glad we made the effort.

We were extremely busy at Easter. We held numerous services in the villages and on the station. We had an unusually large number of visitors. Many missionaries from Zaire (now DRC) who were feeling the strain of recent days of tension, came along to us for a break. We hoped that they would return home refreshed in body, soul and spirit. We then had the usual run of hitchhikers. There were two young geologists who spent the Easter weekend with us. One had been on the road for two and half years and the other for five weeks. They met up in Khartoum and had travelled south together. They were fine, well-educated young men out to see as much of the world as possible before being tied down with life's responsibilities. I felt that their visit to us was no accident. They were keen to attend the Easter Sunday service and were moved by all that they saw. We prayed that a deeper experience would soon be theirs and that they would respond to the love of Christ and His claim on their lives.

Children's Evangelists are Trained

No sooner had we bade farewell to our visitors than we were plunged into a Sunday school teachers' conference. What a joy it was to see over 30 evangelists from distant villages gathered to pray for young people and to be stimulated with new ideas to reach the children with the message of salvation. As I stood before all these fine dedicated evangelists, I could not help thinking of all the fine material aids we had back in England and compare them with our poor makeshift efforts. I was reminded however, that nothing could replace a real love for the children. No amount of material aid could possibly take the place of a personal interest in any individual child. Every moment of our two-day conference was packed with prayer, Bible study and practical lessons. On conference days we ate together, and it was surprising how tasty a large dish of boiled beans could be when the right spices had been added.

We then returned to our normal routine and diet. The secondary school was in full swing with the Bible School as active as ever. We were repeatedly reminded that we had to redeem the time. Events taking place within the framework of the church in Zaire caused us to realise that the doors could be closed to the Gospel at any time. Only a week before, we had heard of an American Pentecostal being expelled from the country having been given just three days' notice.

July was an extremely busy month with schoolwork. We had end of school exams and then we had 100 entrance exams to correct from the young people trying for a place in September. We had to select 25 of the best from that 100. Madeleine Zbinden had finished her contract with the Zairean government and hoped to spend more time in Switzerland. Before she left Bukavu, I went along to spend a weekend with her. The Baptist mission in Congo now had a light aircraft which was due to leave Bukavu to return to Goma empty and I was offered a free journey back to Goma. The following day I came back over to Gisenyi.

New Blessings – a VW Beetle and a Copying Machine!
In late August, I was able to buy a new Volkswagen 1300 beetle. The garages put a protective metal sheet under the body and protective plates under the wings to guard against the loose stones and rocks that could damage it. It was a kind of armoured plating. We had no tarmac roads in Rwanda. Whilst in Kigali I obtained a Gestetner copying machine and this proved to be a great help with exam papers, lectures for the Bible School and lessons for the Secondary School. The instruction manual recommended

that we use blotting paper to dry off excess ink before storing the stencils for future use. We had no means of obtaining blotting paper, but old Swedish newspapers were the next best thing. We would peg the used stencils on a line in a cupboard, so it was easy to choose the one we wanted without rummaging through a stack of stencils. We of course had to be innovative all the time.

A Tragedy that Shook Us
The new term began in mid-September and all 24 students arrived on time! They were a little older but as usual were keen to settle down to work. We taught them French, history, geography, science and mathematics. We did often have to stop teaching history as it was the history of Rwanda and could cause huge tensions in the class due to the ethnic struggles. Just two weeks into the term, the Sunday afternoon calm was shattered by a loud banging on the door. You can imagine our shock when some students announced that one of the lads had drowned in the lake. He was a 17-year-old fine Christian. We had to hire a diver to recover the body. Fortunately, the mining project in town had a diver available and all the necessary equipment needed to recover the body.

Apparently, the lake was full of gas pockets and if you gulped some water in you went down straight away which may have been the cause. The body was recovered on Monday. Dorcas and I together with some Bible School students travelled up into the mountain region to tell the parents and bring them to Gisenyi for the funeral. It was extremely hard going into school seeing an empty place, just two weeks into the term. All the students had been down by the lake when the tragedy took place. It was very painful for them. At the time of the incident, there was a huge football match in the other direction so the people that could have helped were at the football match. The only way we felt we could help was to have a time of prayer with the students and just be with them during such a painful moment.

In the first year of being in Rwanda we used packing cases that were broken down and all different lengths for beds. You really had to use anything you could find and so I raided the shed, having to be innovative. The mattresses were made of banana leaves and grass, and we would stitch two raffia mats together, stuff them with banana leaves and grass for warmth. It was very similar to what we would have had in the air raid shelters back in the war in England.

In the second year of being in Rwanda there was a building project going on and there were spare planks of wood that I could take to use for the beds. I decided to temporarily borrow them. Underneath the planks were cement blocks. If young people stayed in the village, they would have to pay for accommodation, so these makeshift beds were a much better way for people to be able to afford to come for schooling and stay onsite. All the students would have come from different provinces, covering long distances and so accommodation was important.

John and Emy Österberg had returned to Rwanda the year before, after several years, to visit the school. They had been responsible for the work in Gisenyi before Simon Petterson's time but were now pioneering a project in Byumba. They held their first baptismal service in November. When passing through Gisenyi they reported the scene of mocking unbelievers gazing in bewilderment as one after the other passed through the waters of baptism. At the close of the outdoor service, a wave of heavenly silence fell on the crowd and a local evangelist preached God's word to over 1000 men and women gathered to witness the first baptismal service in the area.

Dorcas had now completed a four-year period and so she left for Sweden on furlough in early December. For the Christmas period, Ruth Larsson and I went along to the Kiyove mission. The house there was a similar wooden chalet style like the one I lived in at Gisenyi, overlooking the lake.

On Christmas Day, Ruth ministered in the Kiyove church and I went along to the Rubanga outpost. I arrived back in Kayove in the evening in time to join Ruth who had invited Pastor Paul Buhumbana and his family for a meal. It was a wonderful moment, witnessing the joy on the faces of Paul's five daughters as Ruth lit candles on the table and heard the spontaneous burst of song as they opened their presents. She had, of course, raided the refugee clothing for these little girls who were aged three and above. Later that week I had the joy of ministering in Ruhengeri during the induction service of two new pastors.

God's Financial Provision
During this season in Rwanda, AOG's financial support had come to an end because I was working with a different mission's organisation but Bethel Church in Dagenham continued to send a portion of money to AOG for me. AOG

Boys from the school in Gisenyi helping to cut logs for the kitchen would in turn send the money into my account. The rest of the money I needed to live on was just provided by God in so many different ways! I always remembered the passage in Luke 22:35, *"When I sent you without purse, bag or sandals, did you lack anything?"* No, I lacked nothing! This was a real step of faith as I had no guarantee of finance, but I knew I had the Word of the Lord to stand on and God always provided for my needs

----

Reflect...

So much of this part of Kathleen's story was about God's incredible and miraculous provision in the face of a great step of faith. When was a time you took a step of faith, having to rely only on God's provision? What did that do to your faith in that time?

Chapter 11

Signs of Unrest in Rwanda

1973 - 1975

"There is neither Jew nor Gentile, neither slave nor free, nor is there male and female, for you are all one in Christ Jesus." Galatians 3:28

I mentioned a time of blessing in the churches at Christmas and New Year, but the country as a whole was experiencing political tension. A new wave of violence arose against the Tutsi. Many lost their homes, possessions and even their lives.

Threats in the School

In Gisenyi the term progressed but there was unrest amongst the students. One day I went into class and a message in Kinyarwanda had been written on the board 'blood will flow, and fires will burn'. A clear threat. The students had been warning me that trouble was brewing. Not knowing how to proceed, I asked Ruth Larsson for advice as we were the only two on the mission station at that time. She called for the pastor who promptly came and read the scriptures. He read from Galatians 3:26-28 *"So in Christ Jesus you are all children of God through faith, for all of you who were baptised into Christ have clothed yourselves with Christ. There is neither Jew nor Gentile, neither slave nor free, nor is there male and female, for you are all one in Christ Jesus."* He wanted to emphasise that not only in Christ was there no Jew, nor Gentile but there was also no Hutu, Tutsi or Twa. He reminded the students that they were privileged young men having been given the opportunity to further their education.

At the time, it was estimated that the Tutsi were 9% of the population, the Twa 1% and the Hutu 90%. President Gregoire Kayibanda emphasised the importance of democracy and as the Hutu were the majority tribe, they had the right to rule. Committees began to emerge to check if the Tutsi had exceeded their quota of students in secondary schools, universities or even doctors in hospitals or leading roles in the civil service or in private business. Only a certain number of Tutsi were allowed in these roles and so this was a troubling time for their ethnic group.

One afternoon after school, I noticed that a group of students from a neighbouring school had descended on the mission and were engaged in heated discussion with some of my students. I asked Ruth to come with me and silently pray for peace to rule. We knew that violence could become a likely outcome of these heated discussions. The conversations continued for quite a while and were becoming increasingly tense. Suddenly there was a cloud burst, the heavens opened, and we were all drenched by heavy rain. Ruth and I went into the classroom followed by some of my students and the students from the neighbouring school took refuge on the veranda of my house. Later when the rain ceased and I returned home, I discovered that the students' evening meal that had been simmering on my veranda had been devoured by these neighbours. Despite this I was just relieved that there had been no violence.

That night, under the cover of darkness, the three students thought to be Tutsi who had been singled out by the vigilantes made their way out of the area. I had a class of 30 at the time and so 10% were Tutsi while the 90% were Hutu.

The Bible School was also caught up in this visit, but the only student who was a Tutsi had already been hidden in the woodpile and was later able to find refuge over the border. The President cancelled all the Easter holidays for secondary schools as he feared the students would set light to the villages and cause even more violence. Gradually calm was restored and routine work was able to continue as normal.

Coup D'état and School Holidays Granted

On 5 July, Major General Juvénile Habyarimnana took over the government in a bloodless coup d'état. The next morning, he announced over the radio that the killing must stop and there was to be no ethnic distinction, thus Hutu, Tutsi and Twa were all Banyarwanda. Students' activities were thwarted overnight, and we were granted our summer holidays. The attitude amongst the people was "an order is given so don't think it through, just do it!" It was a huge relief.

Simon and Zelma Petterson had been in Lemera at that time. Their daughter Birgitta and her husband were working in the hospital. It was a very happy time of family celebration for them as not only had their son Lars-Martin come from Sweden to pay a short visit to his childhood home, but Birgitta had given birth to a daughter.

Now that we had been granted our school holidays, I was invited to join friends travelling a little north in Zaire to Beni to visit some Pygmy villages. From there we went to Mount Hoyo where in 1944, caves were discovered, and interest shown in stalactite and stalagmite formations. These caves were only opened to the public in 1957. Nearby there was a picturesque waterfall known as the Venus staircase.

Back in Gisenyi the dry season was well advancing. Just outside my home, there was a well-established flourishing cactus plant. Every morning, white birds that we called tick birds or cattle egrets enjoyed a succulent breakfast and once satisfied by the fruit they proceeded to the nearest herd of cows grazing in the field to peck away at the ticks on the cows.

Our wooden style home needed to be protected from the heavy rain and so some handymen painted the outside walls with spill oil (old car oil). This stopped the rain penetrating the wood. They then went down into the cellar to perform the same task on the floorboards to protect against insects. This operation left a very unpleasant odour for a few days but necessary to preserve the wood. I was told it was as effective as creosote.

A Visit from the President and a Surprise Gift of Shoes!
Not long after the new school year began, President Habyarimnana visited Gisenyi and so there was a fine display and march past. He timed everything just right and at one o'clock, behold, when all the outdoor events ended the rain came down. A few days later, the American ambassador's wife came along to the mission with two pairs of shoes for me. She had seen me at the President's evening reception and thought that they might fit me. Now I was the proud owner of blue and pink shoes - God's provision for special occasions!

There had been a shortage of petrol in the country for several weeks. We were issued with ration cards permitting us to buy 120 litres a month. Despite the ration cards, we could not use them because there was nothing in the pumps. I was glad that a few weeks before Easter, petrol was available again for I had planned to spend Easter with Elizabeth Tobler who had been alone at Karengera since October. Her brother Alfred and his family needed to return to Switzerland for medical treatment. Karengera station was a vibrant station with several outposts catering for schools, churches, and small dispensaries. Elizabeth was expecting another young lady to join her in July.

In late April, Dorcas returned from furlough, and we were glad to see her - not least the Bible School students. Simon and Zelma Petterson were to leave for furlough on the 21st May. They were exhausted having spent the last five years on the mission field. The morning they were to leave, we wondered if they would be able to fly up to Kigali as the weather was so bad and we questioned whether the 'Pippercup,' a very small plane, would be able to take off. But in the afternoon the sunshine came out and we were able to wave them bon voyage.

Breakouts of Disease

Pastor Paul came to Gisenyi to report sad news regarding families in the Kayove area. He had to temporarily close three churches after 70 families lost loved ones due to meningitis and an outbreak of typhoid was threatening.

Local dispensaries were doing all they could to vaccinate and care for the population.

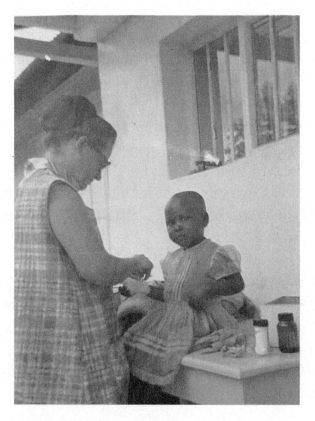

Elizabeth Tobler - one of the missionaries who was a nurse. I spent the Easter holidays of 1974 with her

The school year of 1973-1974 ended on a peaceful note and for me a great surprise. I opened a letter inviting me to visit Sweden during the summer holidays. This invitation included a visit to Gothenburg and Stockholm. I visited some of the churches that were by this time supporting me.

I visited Kaggeholm, a Bible-based college that trained missionaries and pastors and a further education school along with a museum.

School Life Continues

I arrived back in Gisenyi on 21st September in time for the new school year. Imagine my joy when I learnt that the official date for the new term was delayed until 26th September. These few extra days were a real gift. I was able to make new sheets and mattress covers for the boarders, have the dormitory roof repaired and there was even money to have some extra beds made. I praised the Lord that we no longer needed to use the makeshift beds that were installed the year before.

Despite the lack of regular transport, all the schoolboys were back on the station for the first day of term and we were off to a good start. Even the school garden was re-dug and planted during the first week of term. We prayed that the crop would be good as the harvest was ruined in July by heavy rains.

The secondary school class was now in the final year of studies, and we were expecting the Lord to call many of these young men into His service. We were pleased to be able to report that the last third year class that we had at Gisenyi had made the grade. Many ex-students were now teaching in local primary schools and others had found places in local offices. Some students continued their studies. One lad had an important post in the Ministry of Finance!

Many Changes Taking Place

The new church building was beginning to look like a reality and not just a promise. New burnt bricks had been delivered, sacks of cement were waiting in the work sheds and men were breaking up lava for the foundations. By now we had Ezekiel, a Rwandan teacher to help us in the secondary school. The education system was undergoing changes and the school year of 1974/75 was the last under the present regime. A field conference was held in January 1975 as political trends and pressures within the churches needed to be settled. There were a lot of Tutsi versus Hutu hostilities and problems taking place. A lot of prayer was needed. Much time was given to prayer and instruction from the Word of God.

Pastor Gabriel Kapitura, a pastor in Shangugu (now Cyangugu) had been teaching in the Bible School over the course of a week. Unfortunately, his car broke down in Karengera, so he was obliged to thumb a lift to Gisenyi to fulfil his week's teaching appointment. What a blessing it was for him that 26th October was a national holiday. Dorcas and I had been able to travel with him as far as Kibuye where missionaries from Karengera had promised to deliver his car. We arrived late and enjoyed the lakeside tranquillity before making the return trip. We planned to stop at Mabanza in Kayove district for the morning church service as the people there seldom had visits from missionaries.

Sunday Visits to a Variety of Church Buildings
Sundays were taken up with visits to the outstations - what a pot pourri of meeting places! Sometimes in the open air, sometimes in fine burnt brick churches, sometimes in mud and wattle buildings and often in broken down classrooms. I was in such a broken-down classroom one Sunday and the whole building itself left much to be desired, but praise the Lord, the spiritual atmosphere was rich in blessing. Pastor Ephraim's wife was present, and she had been sick for a long time following a serious operation, so there was a real note of praise in the service for her recovery. The room was packed to capacity and all the windows were filled with people standing outside determined not to miss anything. Best of all we could report that people found Jesus! What a blessing that the Lord does not look upon the condition of the church building before blessing lives.

The Generosity from Christians in Other Parts of the World
Practical help was given by the many churches that had been supporting me and they were a great blessing as offerings in the local churches were rarely sufficient to pay salaries for evangelists in the outpost chapels. They relied on the crops from their fields. My home church in Dagenham at one point sent an offering from the women's meeting. This offering covered many costs including a small house for the evangelist at one particular outpost. In Kiyove

there was a main evangelistic post and then nine outposts across the regions. The evangelists would pray and read with the people each day because many could not read, so there was a great need. Four parcels were sent in October 1974, and they had just arrived in April 1975 containing baby blankets and clothing. We were especially pleased to be able to distribute the baby blankets at a dedication service in Kiyove and the clothing to the needy in the area. Once a month they had 'Big Sunday' and all the smaller churches came together. Anyone who had a baby was able to have them dedicated so there were always about 13-15 babies to be prayed over.

During the school year we received 46 sacks of soya milk donated by American Overseas Aid. This addition to the students' diet was a special treat. It was so gratifying at the end of the school year when we were able to announce to the anxious students that all had passed their exams and now could apply for work teaching in the outpost mission school or elsewhere.

A medical check-up in July indicated that I needed an operation. I was to have a hysterectomy. I was assured that the hospital in Kigali had excellent facilities. Indeed, the medical care I received during my 10 day stay proved this to be the case. This all happened very quickly and so I had little time to process that I needed this surgery.

Friday, I saw the doctor. He asked if I was going back to Europe. When I replied "no," he said, "come in on Monday" and the operation was the following day. Meantime, I had to get my own blood! I had to have extra blood but nobody at the mission station had my blood type. I mentioned to the missionaries in Kigali. Then next door the Norwegians did not have any. They went to the Belgium embassy to ask. In the meantime, they went to the Church of England mission office. That day, a lady nurse from Essex, had come to do shopping and she had blood group type O. She heard about it, went to donate blood and then came to tell me.

At the same time, being a nurse, she was the one who told me what exercises I needed to do. She said not to carry anything more than a pound of sugar. I travelled just to go for an appointment and suddenly I was to have the operation. It was performed by a Belgian doctor who spoke excellent English. He had treated many British soldiers during the war. I stayed in hospital for 10 days to recover. I then went back to the mission in Kigali and Dorcas looked after me. I then went back by plane because of the rough condition of the roads. When I got back to Gisenyi I had someone to help look after me. Dorcas went off on holiday.

September was to bring about big changes for me after time recovering from the hysterectomy.

The primary school in Gisenyi where my students would practice their teaching

----

Reflect...

Note how Kathleen is so grateful for the smallest blessings and sees God's hand in everything. What are you grateful for today?

Chapter 12

God's Continued Provision in a New Season

1975 - 1981

'David sang a new song for a new day rises up within me.'
Psalm 40:3

P salm 40:3 which says, *"David sang a new song for a new day rises up within me,"* were words that expressed my experiences at Kayove during the period of 1975-1981. A song with highs and lows. Kayove was a central station led by Pastor Paul Buhumbana but there were nine main churches. Each had a pastor guiding evangelists with the Word of the Lord in the villages.

A New Home with a Beautiful View

Gisenyi mission station had undergone changes in personnel. Ingbert had completed the work on the church building and had moved on to Byumba. Simon and Zelma Petterson had returned from furlough to join Egon Newman and Dorcas in the Bible School. Ruth Larsson had moved out to Kayove. At the close of September, I joined Ruth at Kayove. Our house was situated high up in the mountains and we had a marvellous view of Lake Kivu in the distance. On a clear day we could even see Karisimbi which is one of the volcanoes north of Ruhengeri. We could also see 'Crête congo-nil' where a small stream divides, flowing into Lake Kivu on one side and toward the Nile on the other. I am pleased to say I was much stronger following surgery in Kigali and now engaged in a new endeavour for the Lord.

My new sphere of work would mainly be centred on youth work. Many of the young people in Kayove and the Rutsiro churches were illiterate, so we opened 10 different classes mainly for teenage girls. We aimed to teach reading and basic elements of hygiene and nutrition together with a Bible course. Eventually, the nutrition centres were taken over by the state to try to prevent further increases of 'Kwashiorkor' which is a form of malnutrition caused by a lack of protein in the diet. This condition often caused hair to go grey and skin to be affected. In 1980, Pastor Paul's eldest daughter Perusi was now fully trained and had taken the responsibility of these centres. She received a monthly salary for her services. While home on furlough I had highlighted some of the difficulties that we had encountered in Rwanda. The

Some of the children struggling Kwashior
outside my home in Kayove

support that I received and many answers to prayer
recorded here bring glory to God alone.

Volcanoes, Baboons and Interesting Journeys
In the rainy season, so much could happen when travelling.
The journey into Gisenyi is one of great beauty. You can
travel through a section of the rainforest and the vegetation
is very dense. Early morning or late evening we could be
surprised by encountering a family of baboons. Often

through clearings in the forest we would get a glimpse of the volcanic range and then skirting Lake Kivu we would pass through a modern tea plantation. The road is mostly rough for it was an extinct lava field, then wonder of wonders, the last 10km is a tarmac road into town. All this is picturesque only when the weather is dry. In the rains, our joys were often transformed into tales of woe! On one occasion Ruth and I attempted to travel into Gisenyi for food supplies. We travelled through the rainforest without difficulties but then 20km from Gisenyi the road was blocked by a landslide. Workmen were already trying to clear the road. We decided to wait and see if the road would be cleared before nightfall. We did not need to wait long before Apollinair, an evangelist working in Nyamnyumba area came up to us and advised us to return home. He told us there were six more landslides between Nyamnyumba and Gisenyi, and the workmen had not yet arrived at those other sites. It took a week to clear the roads! When we attempted the journey again, we arrived safely in town but what a welcome we had - heavy rain and at 4pm a cloud burst in a manner I had never experienced before followed by a strong wind ripping metal roofing material from houses in the local township and completely destroying a wing of the mission primary school. We were glad to return to Kayove the following day and to see our little red roof was still in place. On another occasion, we had a unique hailstorm resulting in two broken windows caused by extra-large hailstones that covered the ground for the next two days. They were the size of golf balls! It could get quite cold up in the mountains so at some point I had a chimney built for me so I could have a fire to take the edge off the chill.

Building Works

The mission station was a hive of industry as new buildings were going up and existing ones being renovated. A new seven class primary school was being built. Huge rocks had been hewn from the mountainside by hand and when the local Toyota truck had broken down these rocks were carried native fashion to the building site. Then we had another hillside transformed into a brick and slate field. Mud bricks and slates were laid out in the sun to dry. They were turned daily ready for the brick kiln. We had already burnt over 2000 bricks, and we had a third kiln almost ready for baking. The fires in the kiln had to be fed night and day to maintain a steady supply of heat. In this way, I learnt, the real meaning of 'half baked!' On one occasion a truck load of bricks was ordered only to find them half-baked and so not suitable for building. We had already paid for them so could not send them back. We made sure we knew they were made correctly for future use.

My kitchen was having a face lift or rather a new roof. The water tank was being repaired and enlarged. We had to trust that once the tank was enlarged, there would be sufficient pressure to flush the toilet and have running water in the kitchen. At that time, all water was brought up from the river by the night watchman.

Visits to the Islands and Mountains

One day I sat in the garden and observed a fleet of canoes that had taken advantage of the early morning calm to cross over to the many scattered islands where they would exchange their wares: bananas, beans, manioc, maize, sweet potatoes, peas, oil or even a roll of cheap cotton material could be found at the bottom of the canoe. The men had to make the crossing before noon for afternoon wind and rain could soon whip up the lake surface into dangerous waves. Rugamba church had an outpost on one of the islands. One Sunday, I joined the pastor to minister there. Added to the normal cargo we took two huge parcels of baby blankets and clothing that had been sent out by the Basildon AOG church. Faithful young people in Essex had been knitting and sewing and praying for the work in Rwanda. How glad we were for such practical help.

By 1977, the planned Bible study days were beginning to function. I was out in central churches once every month to preach and teach. We had nine central churches and so that entailed a great deal of travelling and often camping overnight in the freezing mountains. Conditions were primitive to say the least, but it was worthwhile.

In Buganamana, a Rutsiro church we had 77 evangelists gather for Bible studies. Then on the Sunday, we held a gospel service in the nearly completed church. Many crammed into the building with others sitting on the grassy banks outside. There were probably about 2000 people in attendance. One of the missionaries built a little hut for me so I did not have to keep travelling up and down in one day. Some friends from the United Kingdom had given me a camping bed and a sleeping bag that I rolled up and put in my bag.

In Mabanza, we held the half yearly youth rally. Roughly 260 teenagers were present. Many of the youngsters took part in song and even gave a short word. I was amazed to hear them recite whole chapters from the Word of God and even more amazed when the offering was announced. 18,000 Rwanda Francs - the equivalent of 120 British Sterling pounds. We sat out in the open so perhaps this money would be used to build a local chapel.

Fuel Shortages Resulting in Mountain Trekking

Despite a fuel shortage, I was still able to make trips into the mountain regions. In late February, I was granted 30 litres of petrol, just sufficient for the 300km round trip. Then in March, I had 15 litres and with help from other missionaries was able to make a second trip. In April, petrol had dried up again in the tank and my travels had to come to a halt. Outposts were visited on foot wherever possible. I heard that petrol was to be flown in from France but at what price I wondered.

We held a large baptismal service for the whole of the region. I went along to Gacaca, a two hour walk up into the mountains where we baptised 105 candidates. Church numbers were growing and so was the cry for more workers.

I recall visiting Kigamba where the roof of the primary school had blown off. I needed to see the extent of the damage so there was another long trek into the mountains. The young girl on the path ahead of me, had a large basket of potatoes balanced on her head. She seemed to make light work of the climb whereas I was struggling even though people were helping to carry my bags.

A Visit to a prison
Scripture Gift Mission made a very generous donation - four sacks of bible literature and illustrated scripture leaflets printed in Kinyarwanda, French and Swahili. This was a wonderful asset for the evangelists when working in the villages. I, too, had the joy of distributing these leaflets to Sunday school children. At Christmas, the children were delighted to receive a small boiled sweet and an illustrated account of the Good Shepherd as a Christmas present. These tracts were also available for our 'prison chaplain'. We had a pastor in Gisenyi called Pastor Eli who volunteered to go into the local prison. He had good access and support from the wardens. The prison in Gisenyi had 700 prisoners, many of them were 'lifers'. Over the Christmas period of 1978-1979, Eli arranged to take Dorcas and myself on one of his visits. We were given a warning that we were going in at our own risk! As we walked through the heavy metal door, the stench was overwhelming and the ground was wet and muddy, but my greatest memory of that day was the sea of outstretched arms and the voices pleading 'Please let me have one!' referring to the tracts we

Christian books and Bibles given out to the local children

carried. Pastor Eli gave a short gospel message and our visiting hour ended. We were ready to leave when suddenly, a couple of prisoners came with their soup bowls filled with water and there was an impromptu feet washing ceremony. They began to wash the mud off our shoes and to say over and over 'thank you for visiting us!' What a day! It will forever be etched in my memory. It happened to be on a Christmas Day that we had this wonderful experience.

Reading Programmes

The reading programme continued to advance. 'Umuseke', a Kinyuranda word signifying the early light of day was the title of a new series of books that we believed we would soon be able to place in the hands of the non-readers in

Rwanda, the land of a thousand hills. It had been based on the 'Each One Teach One' method. This method was actually created in the USA during the time of slavery when Africans were denied education including learning to read. When an enslaved person learned or was taught to read it became their duty to teach someone else spawning the phrase "each one, teach one."

I think back to Easter 1978 when I casually announced to a group of people that I was willing to teach them to read if they cared to come along after their day's work at the brick kiln or out in the fields. Ten or so young adults arrived. By 1979, I glanced through the registers and there were 60 names recorded in Gihinga, 30 in Gakeri, 100 in Mutabi and so the lists grew in other areas. We ended up with 350 men and women attending reading classes.

I trained the evangelists to also go and teach people using this same method of 'each one, teach one'. I had come to Kayove where I taught them how to teach this method and then they went out to the various villages in the area. We had several who had stumbled and stuttered their way through the first three outdated booklets and so I was able to give them new learning materials. I also used the children's Bible called 'Kera Habayeho' to help people learn to read. It was delightfully illustrated but quite expensive. I am glad I had a happy band of evangelists helping in this reading scheme. I was able to teach this method of learning to read even though I did not necessarily know the different languages or dialects of the people including Kinyarwanda which was the main language. At the time the languages I did speak were Swahili which was the market language and French which was only used by those who were educated and of course Swedish to communicate with many of the missionaries.

God's Provision and Protection

On a fairly regular basis, the main pastors came to Kayove for the elders' meeting with Pastor Paul. When I first visited Mahembe Pastor Shadrack's wife, Esther, told me of the difficulties that they had endured. The land was barren, and their gardens produced little or no fruit. There was great opposition to their work and when the pastor was away from home, the church was broken into. The family suffered theft from their outbuildings and they were often disturbed at night. On one occasion, Esther was alone, and she was praying for peace. That night, there was a loud knocking on the door which obviously caused her great fear. This was then followed by a very gentle tapping. Esther felt compelled by God to open the door even though this would not have generally been the safest or wisest thing to do. When she opened the door, the whole area burst into light. She said that she saw the chariots of God and then she quoted Psalm 68:17 *'The angels were numerous. Thousands times ten thousand.'* And she said to me, "I knew I had no need to worry. The gentle tap was God." What a marvellous account of an angelic visitation! When Shadrack came home, she said to him, 'We've no need to worry, the Lord is around about us!' Her testimony and faith were a great encouragement for me because we had planned to enlarge and build a new church at Mahembe which would eventually be paid for by my home church in Dagenham.

A Short Trip to Sweden Including an Incredible Answer to Prayer

In 1979, I was asked by the Swedish mission/church to teach English at Kaggeholm school during the month of July and was told that all my travelling expenses would be covered. When the pastors heard that I was travelling to Europe in the summer, they asked me to attend the elders' meeting. The meeting proceeded as usual with regional reports and then the outstanding needs and building projects. I was asked if during my time in Europe, I could bear in mind, the following needs: 1. Clothing 2. Communion sets 3. Air mattresses. (They knew when I went to the mountains that this was what I took but when they would come to Kayove they would sleep on the church benches.....air mattresses seemed like a good idea....just like Kathleen!) 4. Money for building work and 5. Sunday school materials.

I explained that I was neither going on furlough nor visiting churches, but I was going to a school to teach English. I decided to encourage them to pray and if anything was given to me, I would bring it back. At that time, I remembered Hudson Taylor the missionary to China and how he reminded people that they can pray, and God can answer them without having to go searching for it. In all honesty I did not expect for these prayers to be answered.

I went on my journey to Sweden via Dagenham. Within a short period of time the prayers began to be answered. When I walked into Bethel, my home church, the Pastor's wife Mavis Jarvis, asked, "Can you do anything with this clothing that we have in the music room?" This was the first greeting I received - the first prayer answered! Then, in the prayer meeting, someone gave me an envelope to be opened later. The envelope had £100. There were air mattresses in the Army and Navy store in Dagenham and each mattress was £10 with a pump and some spare patches. We had 10 men wanting mattresses and so each Pastor got one - another answer to prayer! The Sunday school at Bethel also gave me an offering so I went to the nearby town of Romford and bought stainless steel canisters and flan pastry trays. I bought 21 of them each to be used for communion sets.

A few days later, in the post, came a cheque with a message, "Buy yourself some loaves and fishes." This happened to be the title of new Sunday school material waiting to be printed in Kinyarwanda. Then, of course money for building work came from all quarters eventually. Now the Lord had answered the prayers for all the requests! There remained the problems of metal drums to transport the goods back to Africa. I was invited by the Bexleyheath AOG church in London, for the evening service. At the close of the meeting, I asked if anyone could tell me where I could find some metal drums. Pastor Michael Jarvis from my home church in Dagenham contacted me shortly afterwards and said "Kathleen, I know you were asking about metal drums. The Bluewater cement company in Dartford are willing to help you. They will send the drums to the church, you can pack them and lay cardboard over them, close them and they will come and collect them and seal the lids in place for you." I had to paint my address on the side of the metal drums to ensure they got to the correct location and did not get mixed with cement! One of the leaders at the Bexleyheath church was working at this cement factory at the time. Yet another piece of the jigsaw puzzle of answered prayer was in place.

I went on to visit Beryl Gough in Manchester after a week in London and then onto Sweden to teach for a month before returning to Rwanda.

Battles and Blessings
Although my time in Kayove was one of great blessing, provision, and answers to prayer, it was also full of opposition that I had to battle through. When I was asked to go to Kayove, the Rwandan leaders had it in their heads that I would begin a teacher training college but when they heard a new primary school was being built, they thought they would need teachers and so assumed I would head up the school, but I had to say no. I did not feel that was my calling at that time. I had seen something vastly different and at this point in my life I felt I was called to build up and train evangelists because this was where they needed help. There was a clear clash of vision. They invited me presuming I would do one thing, but I knew I had to stick

true to what God was calling me to do in that season of my life.

I remember on the first night when it became apparent there was a difference in opinion on what I was to do, I laid in bed weeping and asking God if I really still belonged there. Despite this opposition I was able to push through and ensure I was living out my calling.

Reflect...

This chapter speaks a great deal of the amazing things God was doing on the mission field through the work of missionaries and locals. There are a number of times that churches 'back home' are mentioned as having supported the work. Who are you supporting or encouraging around the world in their work for God?

Could you reach out to someone and encourage them today?

Chapter 13

The Challenge of Building Projects

1980 - 1984

"Be strong and courageous and do the work. Do not be afraid or discouraged, for the Lord God, my God, is with you. He will not fail you or forsake you until all the work for the service of the temple of the Lord is finished."
1 Chronicles 28:20

F or a number of years, we were privileged to receive regular programmes presented by Voice of the Gospel (Ethiopia) and Radio Cordac (Burundi) but by 1977, both stations had been closed by their respective governments. Our national radio or Radio

Rwanda had granted us two 15 minute programmes. On Mondays we broadcast in Kinyawanda and on Fridays in French.

Roland Lord, (a missionary from Kigali) our mission radio technician came to Kayove in June 1978 to make some recordings. The young people willingly responded with testimonies and song. Radio Rwanda was still allowing us airtime when François joined the regular staff at Kigali bringing the number to three. In January 1980 he, along with others, attended a workshop that Tanzania arranged by IBRA radio (International Broadcasting Radio, a Swedish radio channel, established in 1948 by the Swedish Pentecostal movement).

Kayove no longer felt so isolated as I had been provided with a radio transmitter and could join the mid-day link up with all the other stations. I carried the transmitter on my travels to the outposts. I connected the sender to an extra battery in the car and then raised the ariel on a roach rod (a fishing pole) that I bought whilst home in the summer of 1979. Even if I was travelling at midday I could pull over to the side of the road, raise the ariel and still communicate with the other stations. If I happened to stop near a village, children gathered and gazed open mouthed at the whole event.

A Few Difficult Days
The sudden home call of three of our leaders will be remembered by us all. Thursday 24th April 1980, one of the

pastors in Gisenyi was killed in a car accident. This was announced on national radio because that is how everything was announced. Pastor Paul and I travelled into town for the funeral on the following day. Living in the tropics, it is not unusual for the funeral to take place within 24 hours. Whilst we were in the church, news came through on the mission link up that Halvard Nilsson, a missionary in Uvira, Zaire, had also passed away suddenly which they believe was from thrombosis. Bengt Erenehall, a missionary in Bukavu had been asked to conduct the funeral service. Saturday morning, the day of the funeral, he made the journey to Uvira. As he stepped out of the car, he collapsed and passed away about two hours later. As so many missionaries and pastors were already gathered in Uvira it was decided that Erenehall be buried in Uvira the following day. It was quite a shock to have three workers die in consecutive days.

Church Building Projects

Four church building projects were undertaken during my stay at Kayove. My home church, Bethel, and the Swedish church Eskiltuna gave continuously towards the cost of building these churches. The main church at Kayove was expanded. Egon Newman had agreed to oversee this project and instructed the burning of the brick kilns and the actual construction. How delighted we were to gather in such a comfortable church. The newly expanded building would seat at least 300 to 400 inside but we would of course have people outside peering in the windows and sitting outside on the ground. Ingebert Rutstedt was happy to guide the building of the church in Rutsiro and to see that all went to plan. He even added a small annexe so that I could camp overnight when I made my monthly visits to Rutsiro and Mahembe which was such a Godsend.

In February 1980, I wrote home, "We are building a new church in Mahembe. At the moment the term 'building' means that we are burning off bricks and fetching rocks and sand. We hope to lay the foundations soon. This work is in the hands of the local pastor Shadrack and members of the congregation." In May 1980, I wrote, "the rains are still very heavy and it's putting the building project back a little. The finishing date will not be as soon as I first thought."

By September I could write "the building in Mahembe is looking like a church and not a heap of building materials." We had new difficulties to overcome. The state was recruiting workers for a large development in the area and were offering better pay than we were. In September a message came to me in Kayove that all our workers had left us high and dry just as we were about to lay the cement floor and glaze the windows. I was devastated.

My Bible reading that morning was, 1 Chronicles 28:20-21, *"David said to Solomon his son, be strong and courageous and do the work. Do not be afraid or discouraged because the Lord God my God is with you. He will not fail you or forsake you until all the work for the service of the temple of the Lord is finished. The division of the priests and Levites are ready for all the work on the temple of God and every willing person skilled in any craft will help you in the work. The officials and all the people will obey your command."* I sighed, "Lord, I need skilled, willing workers." When I tuned into the mission link up at midday Eris Axelsson in Kibuyi announced that she had given pastor Thomas who was also a brick layer a 10-day holiday and he was on his way to Gisenyi by boat. I knew that the vedette (the cruising boat that took passengers) arrived in Gisenyi at 4pm in the afternoon. I did no more than to set off for town. Praise God! When I met Thomas at the port, he agreed to help us. He and a friend met me in town the next morning and we headed off for Mahembe. After a few more minor setbacks we held the inauguration of the church building on 22nd February 1981.

The contents of the drums sent out from England were a great blessing. There was no difficulty in distributing the clothing as I travelled to the various churches. Despite all the material help, a certain undercurrent of opposition was apparent amongst some of the younger men. I became very discouraged. Living alone, becoming discouraged and having no one to talk to allows for the enemy to get in. In many ways, after having been through so much previously, having to deal with all these small things was deeply frustrating. I remember one evening praying, "Lord, send me to another area in Rwanda where they need a missionary. Or even send me to another mission field!"

I was willing to go anywhere at that time. I opened my Bible and it fell open at Psalm 36:8-9, *"They feast on the* abundance of your house. You give them drink from your rivers of delight. For with you is the fountain of life. In your light, we see light." And I prayed, "Lord I'm in a dark place, I need your light." It was as if the Lord said to me, read the book of Ruth and so I picked up my Bible and read Ruth chapter 1, then 2 and then verse 8 and 9. 'Boaz said to Ruth; *"My daughter listen to me, don't go and glean in another field. Stay here with the women who work for me. Watch the fields where the men are harvesting. Follow along after the women. I have told the men not to lay a hand on you. And whenever you thirst, go and get a drink from the water jars that the men have filled."* It was the word that I needed from the Lord. Although this passage of scripture encouraged me, I still asked the Lord for confirmation.

At the weekend, I was once again in Gisenyi. As missionaries we gathered for prayer on Saturday evening. I again sighed to the Lord, saying "Will you give Kenneth Lance, (a man who I knew had a prophetic gift) a word for me?" I heard Kenneth Lance say, "I have heard your prayer, my daughter" - the very words of Boaz. I burst into tears. This was the word of confirmation that I needed. I was convinced that I could continue and even face preparations for the church that was needed in Rugamba before I left for furlough. (The fourth church building to be constructed).

On this new building project, we brought in 50 or 60 cubic metres of rocks, a young carpenter prepared the doors and Simon Petterson promised to have the window frames welded in the workshop at Gisenyi. Benches would be built locally, cement bought, and money was in hand for roofing materials and to pay for the wages of the labourers. A missionary from Byumba would come along from time to time to help Pastor Gaspar. Due to the rains, the actual construction did not begin before I left for furlough in 1981.

During my furlough between 1981 and 1982, I visited several churches, raising money to go towards the building of both schools and church buildings. I am so grateful for

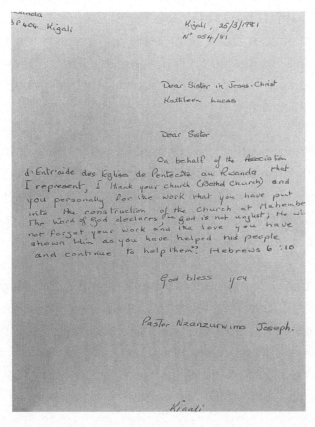

A letter of thanks

the many churches who allowed me to share details about the work and they responded with so much generosity.

Return from Furlough

Following my furlough in September 1982, I was asked by the mission school committee to replace Inger Thereleskog as chaplain to the Protestant students in the Group Scholaire, Byumba. I taught in the school during the week and was in the villages at weekends. School reforms were taking place at a rapid pace. I was in Byumba for just one year and then at the end of the school year, the mission had asked a pastor to take over my post without me knowing about it and requested that I return to Gisenyi because the pastors had expressed a desire for a teacher training school to be established.

Everyone contributed to the building of a beautiful school. In the early summer of 1983, I was offered the job to be the director of the school in Gisenyi which I agreed to. I moved back to Gisenyi in the August of that year to prepare to take over the school.

Dorcas and I were both exhausted and so in August we both took a break. We went to Kigali where I planned to do some business trying to get materials ready for the new school year. From there, we went on to another mission station. We travelled to Kigali via Kayove and Gitarama to avoid the roadworks via Ruhengeri. Kayove where I used to live had been transformed. Stefan and Anita Magnusson had really made a vast improvement to my old home.

Electricity was connected and ran from a little Honda generator. It must have made a difference at night. Stefan was an international radio operator, so he often had contact with Sweden and other places. They would not have been cut off like I was in the days I had spent there.

January 1984: Celebrating my 50th Birthday

It was my 50th birthday on 16th January 1984. The 50th birthday was a great celebration for the Swedish and so at 6am they came into my room with coffee and cakes! I also received another poem written by Zelma Petterson. In the evening, I prepared a meal for everyone, and I was now living in Ruth Larsson's apartment which was a very tiny bedroom and a living room. I had a lovely lace tablecloth in one of the parcels I had received which decorated the table hiding all the holes and I neatly folded the serviettes. I received some wonderful birthday presents from my Swedish friends. I was given a wonderful card saying, "To our Kathleen, 50 years young."

All the missionaries that had known me had written their names and given a gift. What a blessing! One couple had a little five year-old called Thomas. As he ate with me, he said: "You make my chips just like my grandma" and so all the children called me grandma from then on!

My Pet Dogs!

I had a dog back in Lemera called 'Trixie' and in Byumba we had dogs to look after the place especially when I was alone. But one day, I returned from a trip to some of the other mission stations only to find out that all the dogs had died after being poisoned. I was later told that I had to keep a dog in the house so that if people broke in, it would attack the burglars. If they were left outside, people would poison them first and then break in.

I was then given a beautiful pup with a black streak down the back. It grew to be a lovely dog. I asked the children what I should call it and they said in a chorus 'Pluto'. That became his name!

October 1984 brought on another bout of malaria and this occurrence was quite bad. I thankfully came through it and was able to continue with the much-needed work at the school.

Reflect...

Kathleen speaks of a time of great discouragement. Can you think of a time you have personally felt discouragement?

How did you rise above this and are there things you could learn from Kathleen's story to ensure you successfully rise above discouragement?

Chapter 14

School Director & Final Years in Rwanda

1984 - 1992

'One generation commends your works to another; they tell of your mighty acts.They speak of the glorious splendour of your majesty— and I will meditate on your wonderful works. They tell of the power of your awesome works— and I will proclaim your great deeds.'
Psalm 145:4-6

The school system that I was following when I first came to Rwanda, was completely changed by school reforms introduced in 1980. These reforms caused the pastors in Gisenyi, Kayove and Ruhengeri to express their desire for a teacher training school at Gisenyi to meet the need of qualified teachers in all mission primary schools. So urgent was the need that the local officials and tradesmen, helped the pastors erect a three-classroom block. In May 1983, I was asked by the mission's school committee to develop the school and a pastor was engaged to replace me at Group Scolaire, Byumba.

As so often is the case, new beginnings are not without difficulties. For example, the classrooms had wooden shutters at the windows. The aluminium roof left half a panel of transparent roofing material to provide light when the shutters were closed due to rain. The school office was a disused shed with a similar half panel of clear Perspex to give light. I had a table surrounded by wheelbarrows, hoes, machetes, scythes and buckets - material needed for the obligatory weekly 'Umuganda' session - this was the improvement to land i.e. gardening, tree planting and cleaning the main roads. This was a weekly programme initiate by the government and all students were required to participate.

As in 1973, we had difficulties in obtaining books, and teaching material. Being a private school, we were not permitted to buy materials at the education office and there was a limited supply even for official schools. Once again, we borrowed books and the secretary patiently typed stencils and the gestetner machine worked overtime as pages were produced and stapled together. Fortunately, we eventually established a good working relationship with the staff in the education office in Kigali and we were able to buy material and occasionally we were allocated a supply.

Obtaining teaching materials from Europe proved challenging. For instance, in September 1987, I ordered material for the science laboratory. I paid in full for the material and for their delivery. The material was delayed at the border for several months. Finally in April 1988, I received word to say that the material was now released and would be delivered within the next three weeks just in time for the end of the school year.

The Staff

The staff who worked with me at the school

My staff were highly qualified in their chosen subjects. They often made suggestions regarding material needed for their subjects and they even initiated a school magazine entitled, 'Echos de Gacuba II,' a debating society, theatrical productions, and an excellent school choir. This choir was often invited by local churches on Sundays to sing, give testimonies and even preach.

In September 1984, our legal representative invited a young French lady, Claire Badie, to join the staff. We valued her friendship and contribution to the work of 'Gacuba II' and she stayed with us for three years. She lived with Dorcas and myself for a few weeks but then began to have her breakfast and evening meal at home by herself. At Christmas her parents arrived to meet her. It was an answer to prayer because her dad was a plumber and so he set up a shower in Ruth's larder.

Rodolphe was my Vice Principal and his wife Charlotte also worked in the school. I still keep in contact with them to this day.

I, Hannah, will interject at this point to put in some words from Rodolphe regarding Kathleen:

"We do give thanks to the Lord Jesus for placing Mama Kathleen Lucas in our lives. Personally, I met her during the school summer holidays in 1982-1983. She was the brand new director of the teacher training school Gacuba II, Rwanda. Very quickly we noticed that she was a person who

deeply loved the Lord, and she loved her work and paying attention to the personal problems of those who were around her such as teachers or pupils.

As soon as she arrived, she put into practice the morning prayer time. Every morning, before the classes started, we sang a hymn, a song, and read a biblical passage and then we finished with a time of prayer. This continues today - even after the war the school carried on with that morning prayer time. Mama Kathleen had the desire to draw the teachers and pupils to believe in Jesus - it was her responsibility.

Mama Kathleen so enjoyed her work. Her office was still open at 7 or 8pm. She always wanted to ensure she completed the work she had to do. She always paid attention to the personal needs of the professors or pupils. I do remember (I was teacher at that time when she arrived) when I shared with her that I wanted to go and get married in DR Congo where my fiancée was and she offered to buy me a wedding suit.

Her way of getting closer to the people gave her the opportunity to know the families who couldn't pay for the fees to study because they were too poor and so she paid for those pupils. Some of the poorest pupils were working at school during school holidays so they could pay for the fees for the following year. She helped these poorer pupils regardless of what their religion was.

Mama Kathleen was caring of each one of the pupils. When one of them was ill she would drive him or her to the hospital in her own car.

Rodolphe, Charlotte and their family

Charlotte and I wanted to add some other testimonies given by those who were students at that time. Here is what they shared;

"Mama Kathleen was an amazing director. She knew each pupil by name. She would always listen to us and was a real mother to us. That's the reason we gave her the name of Mama Kathleen (meaning Mum Kathleen).

Concerning my family (family Baranyizigiye), Mama Kathleen is still helping us even today. When our oldest son, had to stop his medical studies, we could not afford all the fees, but Mama Kathleen paid for them. She regularly sends the money for fees and it's the fourth year that she has paid for our son Shukrani Daniel. He will finish his study of medicine during the first term of 2022, thanks to Mama Kathleen Lucas.

May the Lord Jesus give her the reward of the righteous in his Kingdom.

Rodolphe - Baranyizigiye Family."

Kathleen and her staff from the school

Cultural Visits for the Students

Cultural visits were encouraged to enhance the understanding of the development within the community. Everything in the community was changing rapidly. I accompanied the 6th form students on their first venture - a visit to a newly developed dairy project. We were offered fresh milk, yoghurt, and cheese to taste. Then we observed the process as milk was sterilised and bottled ready for sale in the local stores. One of the cultural visits was particularly amazing. All Rwandan students were offered a vastly reduced entrance fee on a guided tour to the famous mountain gorillas in the Virunga Park. I readily gave my permission for the staff to encourage the visit for the 13 students.

The government was eager for students to witness what the rangers were doing to explain how important it was to stop poaching. The government wanted the students to understand so as to teach others. The students left at 4am in the morning for this trip, vehicles had to be hired and at 7pm that evening they had still not arrived home – it had been an extremely full day! I was informed that the students went on a long car journey and then had to walk through the rainforest and up into the mountain. They were instructed to be extremely quiet so as not to scare off the gorillas and then if they saw a gorilla, they were to make similar sounds to them and pretend to chew like them which helped them be able to get as close as possible. It was such a fantastic opportunity for the students. Sadly, I was unable to visit but was so glad the students were able to make this trip and tell me all about it after. At some point while I was in Gisenyi a film was made about the famous mountain gorillas and the woman who created it came to stay with us for some time.

More Building Provision

Simon Petterson had a God-given desire to see a teacher training school at Gisenyi. When I returned there in 1983, the first thing he did to help me was to replace the wooden shutters by metal framed glass windows but as he was fully occupied with the Bible School and with the construction of a house for the director of the mission workshop, he could not offer more help at that time. The mission workshop was to be a training school for those who struggled academically and so could focus more on practical subjects such as metal work and woodwork.

When the construction of the house was completed, Simon turned to me and said "oh, if only I had the money, I would build you a simple office and some extra classrooms." I asked how much he needed, and he quoted a sum and I quickly replied: "I have that amount!" I raised the money during my furlough in 1980/81 where I received offerings from churches to cover mission projects. Whilst at Byumba nothing presented itself, but this was the moment to put it to use. The next morning, before I had transferred the money, Simon had staked out a three-classroom block, an office and a small storeroom. By this time, we had between 200 and 300 students, so the extra room was certainly necessary.

This was the beginning of a series of miraculous developments. After 15 months, I was able to move out of the garden shed. The Swedish International Development Aid, SIDA, granted financial assistance to projects throughout the world. The Swedish mission had several projects included in this development aid. Money left in hand at the close of these projects was returned by the mission to SIDA but when Leif Agnestrand saw the amount to be returned, he asked SIDA for permission to use this sum for a school in Gisenyi. It was a vast amount.

The moment permission was granted, containers arrived from Sweden with material for construction work that went ahead at a formidable pace! Accommodation for the girls was built, a dining room, kitchen, solar panel to heat water for the kitchen, a whole administration block, library, staff room, science laboratory, and although the boys remained outside, showers were available for them next to the newly built infirmary.

Even a new primary school was built for the trainee teachers to practice what they were learning. A new house was also constructed for the director with all the "mod cons." We were now electric – I had an electric oven and washing machine! Finally, there was a complete makeover for the original three classroom blocks. So resplendent was the makeover that the fifth and sixth-year students pleaded to return to the classrooms where they began their formation, causing one of the professors to quote an African proverb, "when a wounded animal is about to die, it returns to its origins." The 6th formers were about to suffer their exams!

One of the classes at the school

It had been a long journey, but we do not despise humble beginnings. I was even given a new car! I wrote to my mum, "there are so many new toys to play with that I don't know what to begin with."

Now that the building work was completed, we were encouraged to invite 500 guests to the inauguration on 24th March 1988. Hanging over our heads was still the question of state recognition but despite this, the school was becoming known in the area. The famous art and craft college at Nyundo, asked for their students to come for school practice.

In 1988, the local university asked us to accept a young lady for her final practical exams. Numerous university lecturers came to see her during her month-long stay. We hoped they would speak favourably about us if they were ever approached by the education authorities. This was in April 1988. At the end of the school year, we held our end of year exams and students were about to leave for holiday when suddenly word came that a 'jury central' had arrived. This five-member national examination board occupied our 6th form for a week. The glorious result was that finally our school was officially declared 'Homologué' - officially recognised. Our students now held their well-earned reward after six years of hard work - a state recognised diploma. This would have made a great difference for them in getting jobs in the future. We could all rejoice!

Kathleen in her office at the school

At one point, we had a man come through from the Christian charity Tear Fund. He noticed that we were growing our own vegetables and thought it quite strange. I explained that I was quite happy to grow my own vegetables as it meant we saved money. This man had contact with the charity, "Compassion". He said he would mention to them about our work and he would ask them to contact Tear Fund on our behalf. Eventually I got a letter from Tear Fund asking me to inform them of the number of students I had. They wrote back saying they would provide a grant for all students, money each month for their midday meal. It worked out to be about 15p a day which was half of what I was paying. For a whole year, Tear Fund supported

Some of the students in our school choir

us. Miracles like this just kept happening. One miracle after another - breathtaking!

In these, my final days on the mission field, the blessings were overwhelming. I had electricity and so a washing machine, a shower and so many other things to make life easier. You can imagine how overwhelming it was for me after years without these items.

Unrest in Rwanda

In October 1990, things began to grow worse which was the lead up to the awful genocide. Some days Rodolphe would come into the school and say, "don't ask where such and such a person is as they don't know where their family are." Families were being gradually killed.

The school continued to develop even though there were periods of unrest in Rwanda. In October 1990, the Orevi family and I were evacuated to Burundi for four weeks when Mudende was invaded. We were given the sudden order to leave. I went to Rodolphe, my Vice Principal and told him that we had been told to leave. He told me to just go as I would be seen if something was to happen whereas he and the students could hide in the banana plantations. We had only just started the school term when this occurred, so it was particularly frustrating having to suddenly be evacuated once again.

On 12th February 1991, we were evacuated again when the French troops came to the mission station. The soldiers said that Europeans were invited to join their convoy up to Kigali because Ruhengeri had been overtaken. We were escorted by a convoy of 26 European cars. We did not really know what was happening at the time but were told there was civil unrest. This time I was in Kigali for just a week.

Despite all the unrest, the school continued to function thanks to the African staff. Rodolphe and Charlotte were wonderful colleagues who worked hard with me in the school. There were tensions throughout my time in Rwanda which would eventually lead to the genocide that took place in 1994 just two years after I finally left.

In April 1994 the Rwandan president and Burundian president were killed when their plane was shot down over Kigali. The systematic massacre of the Tutsis would then begin.

I was glad by 1992 that Roland and Anita Hummerdal came out from Sweden to replace me as directors of the school. I felt so confident in leaving the work to such wonderful people and how God protected them through all that was to come. Personally, I was mentally and physically exhausted by this time after so many years on the mission field. After 34 years of service (1958-1992) in the Congo and Rwanda, I was able to retire in April 1992 and return home to Dagenham at the age of 59.

I am amazed as I reflect on the goodness of God throughout my time on the mission field. During times of great difficulty, he protected me and kept me safe. I am so grateful for the people that came my way to serve the Lord alongside me right from the start of my time in Belgium and through to my time in the Congo and onto Rwanda. I am a blessed woman to have been called to serve Jesus in the beautiful countries of the Congo and Rwanda.

'Surely your goodness and love will follow me all the days of my life." Psalm 23:6

Reflect...

It is clear that Kathleen spent considerable time pouring into the next generation so that the school she had led would continue after she left the mission field. Who are you pouring into and developing now to further the Kingdom of God beyond you?

How will you ensure you leave a legacy of faith in others?

Conclusion

1992 onwards

As I, Hannah, write the conclusion to this book, it felt somehow wrong to finish the book with Kathleen's time in Rwanda when she has continued to serve Jesus in so many areas in the local church and further afield. I hope the following words give some understanding of Kathleen's time from the point she returned.

Kathleen returned from the mission field in 1992 just two years before the official start of the genocide in Rwanda. She was mentally, emotionally and physically exhausted. Her dad had passed away which coincided with her return.

Although Kathleen would not want to speak a great deal about this, when she returned, she went into hospital with chronic fatigue. We understand so much more now about mental health than 30 years ago when there was a lack of understanding of "burn out". Mental health was not a topic that was talked about and it was expected in the church world that you would just 'pull yourself together' and keep going.

As you can imagine after years of hard work but with multiple layers of trauma that Kathleen had experienced, we can now understand a little better where this exhaustion would have come from. Kathleen would express that it took her several years to fully recover and regain her strength. I have observed how in doing this project of writing her story it has probably helped her to process some of the pain of what she went through by being able to publicly share it.

Kathleen came home to a very different town than the one she had left. I asked Kathleen how she managed to settle back into a world she no longer knew. She said it was often easier to go back to Africa as it felt more like home to her. She expressed her worry and concern at coming home without knowing where she would live or where she would receive enough finance to survive. Of course, God always supplied but she told me she does not think she had truly learnt to trust the goodness of God for herself personally. On one of her last sessions in talking through this book with me I will never forget her saying, "It is only now that I am learning true surrender to Jesus!" I remember feeling humbled by this statement having written a book of her life being surrendered - I guess we all have so much to continually learn.

Once Kathleen had recovered from her exhaustion, she settled into life back in Dagenham living in the family home with her mum who she would care for until the day she passed away at the age of 99 – Kathleen had the honour of leading her mum to Jesus in the final few hours of her life.

The past 30 years of Kathleen's life have been full of involvement in Bethel Church (now London Riverside Church) in Dagenham. When Kathleen left for the mission field, the church was not at all multicultural reflecting the local area at the time. However when Kathleen returned, Dagenham had changed and developed, with many different ethnicities reflected in the church. I imagine it was a surprise to Kathleen that she found herself having opportunities to help people from the countries she had given her life to. One such example was at a local primary school where my mum worked. It had a Congolese boy who did not speak any English but only French. He was exhibiting extremely challenging behaviour and the school were struggling to know how to handle him. My mum suggested inviting Kathleen in to work with the boy knowing her understanding of the French language. Kathleen quickly discovered that he had been a child soldier in the Congo. Kathleen established instant rapport with the boy and was able to help the school assimilate him. On another occasion Kathleen led an Alpha Course in French as there were a number of Africans from French-speaking countries who had joined the church. Kathleen was able to lead some of these people to Christ through this.

Kathleen was always eager to sign up to any mission's trips that the church put on and so was able to make a number of visits to a church plant we supported in Concarneau, France. Of course, she able to use her French to interpret and connect with people there. She went on three mission's trips to China with the church, a place she could well have ended up going to if she had not gone to the Congo and Rwanda 50 years ago.

Kathleen on a church trip to Israel in 2016

One of the trips I had the privilege of spending a great deal of time with Kathleen on was when we took a team of people on a tour of Israel a few years ago. Kathleen had not planned to go, thinking that the level of walking required might be too much for her. But at the last minute a space became available, and we decided we would help make it work for Kathleen even if she could not do all the walking that everyone else would be doing. As it happened, Kathleen did not want to miss out on anything and so did just as much walking as everyone else and enjoyed the whole experience! I remember asking many questions of her time on the mission field then and being inspired by her faith. For Kathleen when I asked her how she felt about this trip she said to me 'It was the realisation of a lifetime's dream'.

Kathleen has always stood out as a prayer warrior. Kathleen was always in attendance at Prayer Meetings. During the Covid19 pandemic she challenged herself to learn how to do 'Zoom Prayer.' Once she had mastered this new skill, she was then found at every Early Morning Prayer Meeting. She would also stand in prayer when we ran what was called: "The Navigate Course" - a course to help people find freedom. She would attend each session and believe that each person attending the course would find freedom in Jesus. Kathleen said it helped her to unravel some of what she had been through especially when she had burnt out.

During my own days as youth pastor, Kathleen was always a huge support and encouragement to me. I remember taking her into the school she once attended as a student to talk about her experiences on the mission field. Although the school was not in any way a church school, they welcomed a former student who could share information about her work helping other people on another continent.

The students would sit with wide eyes as they listened to some of her stories. I was also incredibly grateful for the way Kathleen continually prayed for and supported the young people I worked with. She always committed to pay for children and young people to come to our kids and youth camps - a sign of her heart for the next generation.

After Kathleen's mother passed away, she moved into sheltered accommodation in the town. Her home is full of pictures and artefacts from her time on the mission field. She made the sheltered accommodation her new mission field and has always looked out for everyone who lives there. During the coronavirus pandemic, a particularly hard time for those living on their own, Kathleen decided to share the gospel with her neighbours. One of her neighbours recently said, "She is the best neighbour I have ever had" – she regularly gives him Scriptures which he now has up on his wall. She has also been able to translate for one of her neighbours who only speaks French.

Kathleen remains close friends with many from around the world that she spent time on the mission field with. She made a number of trips to Switzerland to visit Madeleine Zbinden. She also regularly keeps in contact with Alfred and Lucy Tobler from Switzerland who worked in Rwanda via the phone. She still keeps in contact with Ingegerd Rooth from Sweden and others when she can. I know many of her former students and work colleagues continue to call her.

As you will have read earlier, Kathleen keeps regular contact with Rodolphee and Charlotte who assisted her as she ran the school in Rwanda and continue to run it to this day. As you will have also read, she has supported their son through medical school.

At 88, Kathleen continues to live a full life, continually pouring into the next generation. My hope is that in reading her story many will be inspired just as I have been to give their lives to serve Jesus. I pray that young people will be willing to follow God's call to reach those who others are not reaching - no matter the cost.

Kathleen was an ordinary young woman, from an ordinary, working-class 'Dagenham' family who said 'yes' to follow Jesus wherever He sent her. Will you say 'yes' too?

Kathleen & Hannah as they began writing this book

Appendix 1

Timeline of events of Kathleen's life from birth to the end of her time on the mission field

1934 - Kathleen is born on 16th January

1937 - Kathleen begins attending Sunday school at Bethel Church

1939 - World War II begins when Kathleen is 5. She spends her entire primary school years during the war in Dagenham at Marsh Green Primary School.

1945 - VE Day marks the end of World War 2 on 8th May. Kathleen finishes primary school this year.

1945 -1950 - Kathleen went to Dagenham County High Secondary School (now Sydney Russell)

1946 - Kathleen gave her life to Jesus.

1947 - Kathleen is filled with the Holy Spirit at the age of 13.

1948 - Kathleen is baptised in water at the age of 14.

1950 - Kathleen feels the call to the mission field at age 16.

1950 - 1953 - Kathleen had her first job at an insurance company in London doing paperwork.

1953 - 1955 - Kathleen goes to teacher training college after secondary school.

1955 - 1957 - Kathleen teaches at Henry Green Primary School in Dagenham.

1957 - At age 23, Kathleen goes to Belgium for the colonial course ready to prepare for going on the mission field.

1958 - on 9th November, aged 24, Kathleen travels out to the Congo for the first time to teach at Lemera.

1959 - A visit to Makombo and the field conference for the Congo missionaries. Refugees from Burundi arrive in Lemera due to tribal struggles.

1961 - Kathleen's first escape out of the Congo.

1962 - Kathleen's first furlough after 4 years of being on the mission field and then return to the Congo via a trip to Switzerland.

1963 - Another trip back to the UK for summer and then return to the Congo to direct a school in Lulimba.

1964 - Kathleen along with other missionaries are placed under house arrest for 129 days followed by her 2nd escape out of the Congo.

1965 - Furlough in the UK.

1966 - Kathleen returns to the Congo to the IPPKi teacher training school in Bukavu to train future teachers.

1967 - Kathleen's third escape out of the Congo.

1968 - Kathleen returns to the Congo.

1970 - Kathleen's time in Congo comes to an end after 12 years. She returns to the UK to consider her next steps.

1971 - Kathleen travels out to Gisenyi, Rwanda to work with Swedish missionaries in a school there.

1973 - Unrest in Gisenyi due to tribal tensions.

1975 - Kathleen moves to Kayove, Rwanda to focus on youth work, the training of evangelists and many other ventures!

1979 - A short trip home followed by a trip to Sweden.

1981 - Furlough in the UK.

1983 - Kathleen goes to Byumba as a chaplain at the school there. In September she returns to Gisenyi to become the director of the school.

1992 - Kathleen returns home after 34 years on the mission field.

Appendix 2

Timeline of events in DRC from the 1900's up until when Kathleen returned to the UK[3]

1908 - Belgian control of the Congo begins

1955 - Belgian Professor Antoin van Bilsen publishes a "30-Year Plan" for granting the Congo increased self-government.

1959 - Belgium begins to lose control over events in the Congo following serious nationalist riots in Leopoldville (now Kinshasa)

1960 - Congo becomes independent with Patrice Lumumba as Prime Minister and Joseph Kasavubu as President.

1961 - February - Patrice Lumumba murdered / August - UN troops begin disarming Katangese soldiers.

1963 - Moise Tshombe agrees to end Katanga's secession.

1964 - President Kasavubu appoints Mr Tshombe Prime Minister.

1965 - Army chief Joseph Mobutu seizes power.

---

[3] https://www.bbc.co.uk/news/world-africa-13286306

1971 - Joseph Mobutu renames the country Zaire and himself Mobutu Sese Seko; Katanga becomes Shaba and the river Congo becomes the river Zaire

1973 - 1974 - President Mobutu nationalises many foreign-owned firms and forces European investors out of the country.

1977 - President Mobutu invites foreign investors back, without much success; French, Belgian and Moroccan troops help repulse the attack on Katanga by Angolan-based rebels

1989 - Zaire defaults on loans from Belgium, resulting in a cancellation of development programmes and increased deterioration of the economy.

1990 - President Mobutu agrees to end the ban on multiparty politics and appoints a transitional government, but retains substantial powers.

1991 - Following riots in Kinshasa by unpaid soldiers, President Mobutu agrees to a coalition government with opposition leaders but retains control of the security apparatus and important ministries.

Map of
Democratic
Republic
of the

The location's where Kathleen lived whilst in DRC...

 Lulimba, DRC
1963 - 1965

 Lemera, DRC
1958 - 1962

⭐ **Bukavu, DRC**
1966 - 1970

From Dagenham To Africa with love

Appendix 3

Timeline of events in Rwanda from the 1900's up until when Kathleen returned to the UK

1916 - Belgian rule begins

1946 - Ruanda-Urundi becomes UN trust territory governed by Belgium

1957 - Hutus issue manifesto calling for a change in Rwanda's power structure to give them a voice commensurate with their numbers; Hutu political parties formed.

1959 - Tutsi King Kigeri V, together with tens of thousands of Tutsis, forced into exile in Uganda following inter-ethnic violence.

1961 - Rwanda proclaimed a republic.

1962 - Rwanda becomes independent with a Hutu, Gregoire Kayibanda, as President; many Tutsis leave the country.

1963 - About 20,000 Tutsis are killed following an incursion by Tutsi rebels based in Burundi.

1973 - President Gregoire Kayibanda ousted in military coup led by Juvenal Habyarimana.

1978 - New constitution ratified; Habyarimana elected as President.

1988 - Some 50,000 Hutu refugees flee to Rwanda from Burundi following ethnic violence there

1990 - Forces of the rebel, mainly Tutsi, Rwandan Patriotic Front (RPF) invade Rwanda from Uganda.

1991 - New multi-party constitution promulgated.

1993 - President Habyarimana signs a power-sharing agreement with the Tutsis in the Tanzanian town of Arusha, ostensibly signalling the end of civil war; UN mission sent to monitor the peace agreement.

1994 - April - Habyarimana and the Burundian president are killed after their plane is shot down over Kigali; RPF launches a major offensive; extremist Hutu militia and elements of the Rwandan military begin the systematic massacre of Tutsis. Within 100 days around 800,000 Tutsis and moderate Hutus are killed; Hutu militias flee to Zaire, taking with them around 2 million Hutu refugees. / Refugee camps in Zaire fall under the control of the Hutu militias responsible for the genocide in Rwanda.

1995 - Extremist Hutu militias and Zairean government forces attack local Zairean Banyamulenge Tutsis; Zaire attempts to force refugees back into Rwanda. / UN-appointed international tribunal begins charging and sentencing a number of people responsible for the Hutu-Tutsi atrocities.

Map of
Rwanda

The location's where Kathleen lived whilst in Rwanda...

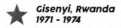

**Gisenyi, Rwanda
1971 - 1974**

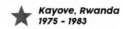

**Kayove, Rwanda
1975 - 1983**

Printed in Great Britain
by Amazon

86333768R00159